That we all might be found...

In Him

on that great day!

Author H. Roye

H. Roye

Published by
Amazon Kindle Direct Publishing
Printed in the United States of America

H. Roye

Acknowledgements

First and above all I would like to thank my Lord and Savior Jesus Christ and express my deep gratitude for His blood that He willingly offered on the cross for me.

I would also like to express how very grateful I am to Terry Williamson, my editor, for all the time and love she poured into me personally, and this book. She was so careful to encourage and not overwhelm me in the editing process.

I am very thankful to my dad, Dan Waite, for his thoughts and encouragement. Thank you for always being there to support and encourage my dreams and life goals!

I was also blessed to have my friend Rebecca Nighswonger and Angela Sudduth's help and encouragement. They spent hours helping me to clarify and implement edits, for which I am extremely grateful.

I would also like to thank my daughter Abigail for her cover design which exceeded my expectations! You did an amazing job Ab! I love it!

I am thankful to many more for their emotional support and encouragement as I worked on this project.

H. Roye

Table of Contents

PART 2

PART 3

PART 4

Introduction

This book was written to feel like a kind and respectful conversation between friends. I felt that with a controversial, difficult topic like salvation, it would be more engaging and allow the reader to be able to gently digest what was being written.

It is my hope that this book will come across in a loving and yet very factual manner. Love is very important in any discussion; however, we must also have logic and facts if we are ever to get beyond our feelings on a particular subject and instead examine God's feelings on the matter as expressed in His Word. We can then stand with confidence on that *Great Day* knowing that we have been washed in the blood of our Savior and clothed in Christ. God no longer looks upon us and our sin, but upon the perfect blood of Jesus Christ! What a wonderful, perfect place to be! So please find a comfortable chair and let's begin our examination of the Scriptures and discover what God's remedy is for our sin and how we can be made perfect in His sight. After all, on that *Great Day,* only God's words and instructions will matter!

Jeremiah 20:9
Then I said, "I will not make mention of Him,
Nor speak anymore in His name." But His word was in my
heart like a burning fire shut up in my bones; I was weary of
holding it back, And I could not.

John 6:68-69
But Simon Peter answered Him, "Lord, to whom shall
we go? You have the words of eternal life. Also we have
come to believe and know that You are the Christ, the
Son of the living God."

How well would it be for our souls now, and on that
Great Day, when God will judge the living and the dead,
if we were to boldly proclaim these words of Peter and
steadfastly live by them? Jesus, Himself, puts the highest
honor on the words of God in His conversation with
Satan when He was being tempted.

Matthew 4:4
But He answered and said, "It is written, Man shall
not live by bread alone, but by every word that proceeds
out of the mouth of God."

Jesus could have just as easily declared that if the word
of God speaks plainly on a subject, that should end all
questioning on that subject. Your position on that
subject should now be firm and settled as every word of
God is true and ought to be accepted as conclusive and
the end to all debate. We should refuse to give up a
single word of the Bible as it alone is our lamp and guide
through this life into the next.

What if the Word of God says something that you don't
happen to like? What if it says something that
contradicts what is being taught and proclaimed in the
religious world as truth?

Will you cling to God and His words, or will you find the honor and approval of man a greater treasure?
The Bereans didn't even accept the apostles' word as truth. They searched the Scriptures daily to see if what the apostles taught was in fact truth from God.

Acts 17:11 (NIV)
Now the Berean Jews were of more noble character than those in Thessalonica, for they received the message with great eagerness and examined the Scriptures every day to see if what Paul said was true.

Will you deny yourself something that you very much want to do and sacrifice it to your Lord, or will you find the love of this world too great? Jesus gave every proof to the Jews that He was the promised Messiah, and yet with hard hearts, they remained unmoved and unbelieving. As the adage says,

---

Unbelief does not arise so much from a want of evidence as from want of will to believe!

Do you have a will to believe the Words of God? Will you say as David did in Psalms 119?

Psalm 119:2-11
Blessed are those who keep His testimonies,
Who seek Him with the whole heart!
They also do no iniquity;
They walk in His ways.
You have commanded us
To keep Your precepts diligently.
Oh, that my ways were directed
To keep Your statutes!
Then I would not be ashamed,
When I look into all Your commandments.
I will praise You with uprightness of heart,
When I learn Your righteous judgments.
I will keep Your statutes;
Oh, do not forsake me utterly!
How can a young man cleanse his way?
By taking heed according to Your word.
With my whole heart I have sought You;
Oh, let me not wander from Your commandments!
Your word I have hidden in my heart,
That I might not sin against you.

We can see by David's declaration to God that He loves God's Words and is committed to knowing them and living by them. Will you commit yourself to knowing God's Words, all of His Words?

I love the following quote from J.C Ryle,

"Man does not search the Scriptures! They do not dig into the wondrous mine of wisdom and knowledge and seek to become acquainted with its contents. Simple, regular reading of our Bible is the grand secret of establishment in the faith. Ignorance of the Scriptures is the root of all evil!"

We do this by committing ourselves to set aside our feelings and prior ideas and to honor God by honoring His Words. We do this by keeping, teaching and living only His Words!

What is the way to heaven? We must humbly submit ourselves to our God and His Words. We must sit at His feet and by faith learn His statutes and His Words. We must love His Words and praise better than the love and praise of men. As we begin this journey together to discover how we are to be found *In Him* and you find that you do not like some of the answers we find, will you humble yourself and submit to God because He is God?

Let's begin our journey together and search the Scriptures diligently to see if these things are so!

Greetings to a Friend

Dear Friend,

I hope this finds you well and enjoying thoughts of the great adventure that you are about to embark on. You are so right about choosing to live for God, that He might use your willingness to bless others and lead them closer to Him. The Word of God is so amazing and full of more wisdom and knowledge than we could possibly grab hold of in our short lifetimes. Let us never stop trying and seeking those things that are above...

Colossians 3:1-4
"If then you were raised with Christ, seek those things which are above, where Christ is, sitting at the right hand of God. Set your mind on things above, not on things on the earth. For you died, and your life is hidden with Christ in God. When Christ who is our life appears, then you also will appear with Him in glory."

So, please grab your favorite cup of tea or coffee (I am enjoying a cup of coffee as I write). This letter will be long and full of many important topics that I hope will keep you steadfast and grounded in the truth of God's word as you endeavor to take it to the world to seek and save the lost, to the glory of God and for His kingdom's sake.

I love thinking of what your life will be like as you steadfastly seek God's will. I am confident that you will be a joy and a blessing to all who are around you. I am sure that they will see the love, peace, and joy in your home, and it will inspire them to seek God more fervently. I look forward to our time spent together. I love your sweet, gentle heart that is set on fire for the Lord! May you always lead your family to be an *Isaiah 8:18-20* family!

Powerful Warnings

Isaiah 8:18-20
Behold, I and the children whom the LORD hath given
me are for signs and for wonders in Israel from the
LORD of hosts, which dwells in Mount Zion. And
when they shall say unto you, Seek unto them that have
familiar spirits, and unto wizards that peep, and that
mutter: should not a people seek unto their God? for the
living to the dead?
To the law and to the testimony: if they speak not
according to this word, it is because there is no light in
them. KJV

I would like to point out to you verse 20. Are you
wondering, what is so important about verse 20? Let's
read it again.

To the law and to the testimony: if they speak not
according to this word, it is because there is no light in
them.

We could ask a lot of questions at this point. Some of
them might be, "Who is this verse speaking to?", "What
Word must they speak according to?", and "What does
it mean by, "there is no light in them?" What do you
think? Especially with regards to, *there is no light in them.*

Thankfully, God restates this same message in the New
Testament, and we can see that He is speaking of His
commands and His Words being honored and obeyed
above man's. Our Lord is serious about His message

being proclaimed, not the ideas and doctrines of men.
We are told here that if we are teaching, we'd better be
teaching God's Words and doctrines. Otherwise, we are
not in the light, but darkness. God is light and we want
to be in the light and to have the light dwell in us. So, it
is very important that we *speak according to His Word!* The
following verses from the New Testament serve to
reinforce that God definitely has not changed His mind
with regards to His desire to have His Words honored
and obeyed over man's.

Mark 7:7
And in vain they worship Me,
Teaching as doctrines the commandments of men.

2 John 1:9-10
*Whoever transgresses and does not abide in the doctrine
of Christ does not have God. He who abides in the
doctrine of Christ has both the Father and the Son. If
anyone comes to you and does not bring this doctrine, do
not receive him into your house nor greet him;*

1 Timothy 4:16
*Take heed to yourself and to the doctrine. Continue in
them, for in doing this you will save both yourself and
those who hear you.*

Galatians 1:8-9
*But even if we, or an angel from heaven, preach any
other gospel to you than what we have preached to you,
let him be accursed. As we have said before, so now I
say again, if anyone preaches any other gospel to you
than what you have received, let him be accursed.*

Please note that God mentioned twice in Galatians that if anyone preaches any gospel other than that which is found in the word of God, that person is ACCURSED! Wow! This is a serious warning to drive home the importance of God's word being defined by God's word and not by man's thoughts or ideas.

PART 1

Doctrines of Men

I have never been a person to beat around the bush, so I will just plunge ahead here and tell you that I am concerned by what some are teaching today. My concern is centered around such notions as "We are saved by grace ALONE", "Just ask Jesus into your heart", "Belief ALONE saves", and "Pray the sinner's prayer and be saved", implying that one is saved, washed of their sins, and put into Christ if they pray this prayer. Let me ask, "What passage in the Bible teaches this doctrine as God's plan for man's salvation?" Let's jump right into a serious study of "What must one do to be saved, have their sins washed away and be put into or clothed In Christ." I pray that you will agree with me that this is a matter of life and death, and therefore, well worth the study and effort that we put into understanding salvation and what it means to be *In Him* as taught by Jesus and His apostles, in His Word.

As we seek God and study His Words, may we always be guided by *all* of His Words! Men throughout the ages have picked and separated those principles and commandments in the word of God that they liked or preferred, and taught those ideas to the exclusion of the other commands and principles found in the Word of God. God wrote one book for all ages and for all people, containing everything pertaining to life and godliness; everything we need in one small book. *Only God could have done this!* Man's volume of an equivalent book would be thousands of volumes and reach to the moon and back again.

God clearly wants ALL of His Words to be equally valued, obeyed and respected by His children. He has not contradicted Himself in His Word and He would have us to love and follow all that it contains no matter what the world or anyone else would say or teach! Our love for the Words of God ought to be so great that we are always willing to give up everything to follow after Him and His teachings.

Dear Friend, please ask yourself this simple question, "If this study should reveal to me that I am not obeying all of God's commands, am I willing to change my thinking, repent, and honor God's ords over my own thoughts and desires?" There is only one thing in this life that I am one hundred percent confident of and that is this, there is a God and someday I will stand before Him and give Him an account of my life! (Matt.12:36, Rev.20:12)

Live by Every Word of God

Proverbs 21:30
There is no wisdom nor understanding nor counsel
against the LORD.

Psalm 119:160
The sum of Your word is truth,
And every one of Your righteous ordinances is
everlasting. KJV

Jesus clearly taught the importance of living by every Word of God and teaching all of His truths together. The sum of His Word is truth and includes what He desires from us. I would also like you to consider that the above passage Proverbs 21:30 states, without apology, that no matter how wise someone might be, if what they have to say is different from what God's word says, it is not wisdom. Neither is it wisdom to only follow part of God's directions. He wants us to follow every word!

Matthew 4:4
But he answered and said, "It is written, 'Man shall
not live by bread alone, but by every word that proceeds
out of the mouth of God.'"

We are to live by every word that proceeds from the mouth of God. So, as we continue through this study, please remember we will not be focusing on one part of God's word over other parts. Nor should we try and make one part of God's Word contradict another part of God's Word because we are to live by every word! All of what God has given us in His Word fits together like a priceless and rare painting! Every word has equal importance! To leave out some of His Words is to destroy His beautiful work of art! After all, we are reading and studying God's Word! May we always receive them and value them as such!

1 Thessalonians 2:13
For this reason we also thank God without ceasing, because when you received the word of God which you heard from us, you welcomed it not as the word of men, but as it is in truth, the word of God, which also effectively works in you who believe.

We are to receive the Word of God for what it is, a *God-breathed* message to man that within itself holds the message of truth. As we study through the Bible together and come across something that we do not feel is clear or we simply do not understand, we need to search to find the context and understanding of the verse in God's Word; thus, letting God define His own Words and concepts.

We need to diligently search to find how God is using and defining words and concepts that we are studying. We should be careful not to read into God's Word with our own preconceived ideas but to simply take what He says at face value.

The gospel of John clearly tells us that the Word of God is Jesus Christ.

John 1:1
In the beginning was the Word, and the Word was with
God, and the <u>Word was God</u>.

Just as your words express who you are, so God's Word expresses who He is. He has chosen to reveal Himself to us through His Word. We should try hard to understand and come to know Him by being in His Word, and never be so conceited as to think that we can add to or subtract from God's Words.

Proverbs 30:6
Do not add to His words
Or He will reprove you, and you will be found a liar.

Yikes! Proverbs strongly drives home the respect we are to have for God's Word. It also provides a sharp warning against adding our own word to His. It's almost as if God knows that adding and taking away is man's tendency. Funny, isn't it? This is exactly what man has done through the centuries: adding this little doctrine and that little practice until there are a lot of religious groups that no longer resemble the church we find in the New Testament. It is very important that we choose to sanctify and honor God's Words and not add to them.

Revelation 22:18
For I testify unto every man that hears the words of the prophecy of this book; If any man shall add unto these things, God shall add unto him the plagues that are written in this book. KJV

John 17:17
Sanctify them by Your truth. Your word is truth.

If we truly desire to seek truth and please God, then we will carefully read and follow what we find in the Word of God. Keep in mind that if you purchase an Apple computer, you do not skim your PC owner's manual and expect to learn how your new computer works and functions. In the same manner, remember that it is God who created us and designed His Church. We should study His manual (The Bible) for answers about ourselves and His Church.

God declares His whole Word to be truth, not one verse we like here and another one that seems great over there. Truth is found in *every word that proceeds from the mouth of God* (Matt.4:4). So, let's not play *operation* with the Words of God, surgically choosing the parts that we like and removing the parts that we don't like or that don't seem to fit with our current beliefs.

Consider how well that would work with your computer. What happens if you decide to ignore the instructions in the owner's manual, simply because you think that the computer should function the way that you decide? You are going to end up with a very messed-up computer. The same is true when we consider doing things our way or some other man's way over God's design as found in His Word.

John 12:50
And I know that His command is everlasting life.
Therefore, whatever I speak, just as the Father has told
Me, so I speak.

Jesus declares in this passage that God's commands are *Everlasting life.*

Do you desire everlasting life? I know that you do! God's commandments are *everlasting life*, all of His commandments. We ought to be saying as Jesus did in this passage that, *even as the Father said unto me, so I speak.* We need to do the same, speaking only as the Word (Jesus Christ) speaks.

Remember that the *sum of His Word is truth* and we are to live by *every Word of God*. May we always examine ourselves to make sure that we are living by every Word of God, and that we are not honoring and obeying some of His commands over others. Truth is only truth when it is complete! If we only have and teach part of the truth, it is not truth at all. Let us…

2 Corinthians 13:5
Examine yourselves, whether you are in the faith; Test
yourselves. Do you not know yourselves, that Jesus
Christ is in you? —unless indeed you are disqualified.

Let us remember God's solemn warning to preach *His Gospel* so we will not be *accursed/disqualified.*

Galatians 1:8-9
But even if we, or an angel from heaven, preach any other gospel to you than what we have preached to you, let him be accursed. As we have said before, so now I say again, if anyone preaches any other gospel to you than what you have received, let him be accursed.

H. Roye

Ask Jesus into Your Heart?

Are the *Sinner's Prayer*, *Grace alone*, *Faith only*, and *Asking Jesus into our hearts* God's plan for our salvation? Do Jesus, His apostles, and the Word of God (which is Jesus Himself, Jn.1) teach these doctrines as the method by which we are saved?

We need a much bigger No!

No… No…No…. Not one of these commonly used phrases (teachings) is found in God's word. They are twisted and words are added to them. Are you thinking, well what's the big deal about adding one little word? Consider; that is exactly what Satan did in the Garden of Eden. He simply added one little word to God's Words. He said, "You shall **NOT** surely die." That one little word deceived Adam and Eve and brought sin and death into the world.

Are you shocked? Are you offended? I pray that you are not, but that you will be that soft and fertile soil that is willing to *search God's word diligently to see if these things are so*. Such were the Christians in the city of Berea. Notice they realized that the answers were to be found in the scriptures. Will you diligently study with me? Shall we seek God in His word together to see if these things are so?

Acts 17:11

These were more fair-minded than those in Thessalonica, in that they received the word with all readiness, and searched the Scriptures daily to find out whether these things were so.

I fervently pray that you will be found in like manner as the Christians of Berea. That you will see the importance of comparing all the doctrines and teachings of men with the scriptures and where they differ, that you will be found on God's side not man's. Also, notice that in Acts 17:11, we are not told to "pray about the doctrines being taught and see what God reveals to us." If God has already spoken about a matter in His Word, He is not going to be giving any ONE man some different, private interpretation.

2 Peter 1:20

Knowing this first, that no prophecy of Scripture is of any private interpretation.

Well then, what does God's Words teach about how we are to be put *in Christ?* How are our sins washed away? As it was asked so many times in the scriptures, *What must we do to be saved?* Jesus Himself and His followers answered this question openly. I believe that we would do well to heed their answer!

I would like to present to you what the Bible teaches as the gospel's plan for man's salvation. I would beg you to consider that God is… well God. If He states something in His Word that you don't like or that is not popular, will you be His dear child and obey Him because He is God?

A good starting point is always the foundation. In the case of salvation, that foundation is the blood of Christ and the importance that the scripture puts on His blood. I sincerely thank you in advance for having the kind of heart to truly read and examine what I am presenting to you out of the Word of God. Please, if you disagree, what scriptures would be applicable to what you believe? Let's sharpen each other and by the grace of God, learn from our studies together!

There is Power in the Blood

The word of God clearly teaches us that we are saved by the blood of Christ. Without the shedding of His blood to wash away our sins, we could not lay hold of salvation. So, no matter God's mercy and grace, we would not be saved without the blood of Jesus Christ. The Bible gives us such a beautiful picture of the Love of God, in that He was willing for His Son to shed His blood for us.

John 3:16
For God so loved the world, that He gave His only begotten Son, that whosoever believes in Him should not perish, but have everlasting life.

The Bible paints us a very clear picture on the importance of blood. From the very beginning, God told His people that the Life is in the blood, both spiritually and physically.

Leviticus 17:11 & 14
For the life of the flesh is in the blood, and I have given it to you upon the altar to make an atonement for your souls: for it is the blood that makes an atonement for the soul....
For it is the life of all flesh. Its blood sustains its life.

Deuteronomy 12:23
Only be sure that you do not eat the blood, for the blood is the life; you may not eat the life with the meat.

Hebrews 9:22b
Without the shedding of blood is no remission.

1 John 1:7b
The blood of Jesus Christ His Son cleanses us from all sin.

Revelation 1:5c
To Him who loved us and washed us from our sins in His own blood.

Exodus 12:13
And when I see the blood, I will pass over you, and the plague shall not be upon you to destroy you, when I smite the land of Egypt. KJV

Revelation 12:11
And they overcame him (Satan) by the blood of the Lamb, and by the word of their testimony.

Hebrews 9:14
How much more shall the blood of Christ, who through the eternal Spirit offered Himself without spot to God, cleanse your conscience…

Hebrews 10:19, 22
Having therefore, brethren, boldness to enter into the holiest by the blood of Jesus … Let us draw near with

a true heart in full assurance of faith, having our hearts sprinkled from an evil conscience and our bodies washed with pure water.

Hebrews 13:12
Therefore Jesus also, that He might sanctify the people with His own blood, suffered outside the gate.

Colossians 1:13-14
He has delivered us from the power of darkness and conveyed us into the kingdom of the Son of His love, in whom we have redemption through His blood, the forgiveness of sins.

Romans 3:25
Whom God hath set forth to be a propitiation through faith in His blood to declare His righteousness for the remission of sins that are past, through the forbearance of God.

Here are some more Scriptures on the importance of the blood of Christ, and the role that it plays in our lives and our salvation. Please take the time to read and meditate on these verses and the significance of the blood of Jesus Christ that was shed on the cross for all mankind. As you read through the passages below, notice the important things that the Word of God tells us that Jesus's *blood* does for us.

Matthew 26:28 remission of sins
Acts 20:28 purchased the Church
Romans 3:25 propitiation (atonement)
Romans 5:9 justified (declared or made righteous)
Ephesians 1:7 redemption, forgiveness of sins
Ephesians 2:13 brought near to God
Colossians 1:14 redemption, forgiveness of sins

Colossians 1:20 reconciliation, made peace
Hebrews 9:12 obtained eternal redemption
Hebrews 12:20 makes us complete in every good work
Hebrews 13:12 sanctify us
1 Peter 1:8-9 redeemed
Revelation 5:9 redeemed
Revelation 7:14 washed

I think that you will agree with the Word of God that the blood of Christ is very important and without it, God's grace would not save us! A quick overview of these verses shows us that blood remits sin, gives life, and allows us to dwell "in Christ." It is how Jesus purchased the church, why Jesus is our atonement through faith, it justifies and redeems, it brings those who are far off to God, forgives sins, reconciles us to God, gives us redemption, cleanses us of our old self and sin, allows us to come before God with boldness, sanctifies, makes us complete to every good work, it is how we are washed, and gives us victory over Satan! I hope that your mouth has fallen open as mine has and that you are saying, Wow! There is power in the blood!

Now we can stand before a righteous God and He no longer sees our sins, but He sees only the righteous blood of our Savior, Jesus Christ! And just like the blood around the doorway of the Israelites' houses, He will see Christ's blood on us and pass over our sins! *Exodus 12:13*

What Can Wash Away My Sins?
Nothing, but the Blood of Jesus!

Now that we have clearly looked at the role of the blood and specifically that the blood of Jesus Christ cleanses our sins, what does the Bible tell us to do to be brought in contact with that blood? The Israelites had to paint blood on their doorpost for it to save them from death. Does that mean that the Jews that obeyed and painted the blood on their doorposts earned, worked for or deserved the salvation from death that the painting of the blood provided for them? Now would be a good time to really answer this question for yourself; so did the Israelites earn, work for, or deserve their salvation from death in the painting of the blood? Before we go on, please take a minute to answer this question.

I hope that we can agree that the scripture and reason would resoundingly say, *"Of course not!"* The salvation from death in the painting of their doorposts with blood was a gift from a generous and loving God who chose to save them if they believed and obeyed. Well then, what if someone believed yet chose not to paint their doorpost with blood? Would their belief save them? Why not? Because, if they truly believed that the angel of death would only pass over them if their doorpost was stained with blood, then that belief would cause them to act and stain their doorpost with blood.

Did their action of staining their doorpost with blood save them? Yes and No. Yes, because God requires man's belief to be an active obedient faith and no, because God choosing to see the blood and Passover was pure grace on God's part and completely undeserved.

I want you to realize that we have the same question before us today. What would God have us do to be washed or covered in the saving blood of Christ?

Romans 6 is very detailed on the subject of how we are bought in contact with the death of our Savior and His blood. On pains of being extremely repetitious, if we find in this passage that we are asked to do something to be put into contact with the blood of Jesus Christ, remember that our obedience and actions simply put us into the same position as the Israelites who obeyed. We in no way earn, work for, or deserve our salvation from death. God is very clear throughout His Word that there is nothing that we could do or give to Him that He needs. So, the idea of earning, working for, or deserving anything from God is quite absurd. God reminds us many times in His word that we deserve or can earn nothing from Him. Our obedience is not payment for our sin nor could it ever be. Only Christ's blood is able to justify us and pay for our sins. Here is the way the Word of God puts the absurdity of us working for our salvation.

What Could You Give
in Exchange for Your Soul?

Acts 17:24-30

*God, who made the world and everything in it, since He
is Lord of heaven and earth, does not dwell in temples
made with hands. Nor is He worshiped with men's
hands, as though He needed anything, since He gives to
all life, breath, and all things. And He has made from
one blood every nation of men to dwell on all the face of
the earth, and has determined their pre-appointed times
and the boundaries of their dwellings, so that they
should seek the Lord, in the hope that they might grope
for Him and find Him, though He is not far from each
one of us; for in Him we live and move and have our
being, as also some of your own poets have said, 'For we
are also His offspring.' Therefore, since we are the
offspring of God, we ought not to think that the Divine
Nature is like gold or silver or stone, something shaped
by art and man's devising. Truly, these times of
ignorance God overlooked, but now commands all men
everywhere to repent.*

Please take careful notice of verse 25

*Nor is He worshiped with men's hands, as though He
needed anything, since He gives to all life, breath, and
all things*

Micah 6:7–8
*Will the LORD be pleased with thousands of rams,
Ten thousand of rivers of oil? Shall I give my firstborn*

38

for my transgression, The fruit of my body for the sin of my soul? He has shown you, O man, what is good; And what does the LORD require of you, But to do justly, To love mercy, And to walk humbly with your God?

In verse seven, the writer declares that there is nothing you could give to remove the sin from your soul, not even your own child! That groundwork being laid, the writer goes on to tell us in verse eight that God does require that we choose to *do justly, love mercy and walk humbly with your God.* Again, remember, just because God requires action/obedience from us, this in no way earns us the right to be *cleansed of the sin on your soul.* The passage is very clear. Just because God requires our obedience does not mean that we earned such a great and wondrous gift from our Creator.

Deuteronomy 10:12-21
And now, Israel, what does the Lord your God require of you, but to fear the Lord your God, to walk in all His ways and to love Him, to serve the Lord your God with all your heart and with all your soul, and to keep the commandments of the Lord and His statutes which I command you today for your good? Indeed heaven and the highest heavens belong to the Lord your God, also the earth with all that is in it. The Lord delighted only in your fathers, to love them; and He chose their descendants after them, you above all peoples, as it is this day. Therefore circumcise the foreskin of your heart, and be stiff-necked no longer. For the Lord your God is God of gods and Lord of lords, the great God, mighty and awesome, who shows no partiality nor takes a bribe.

He administers justice for the fatherless and the widow, and loves the stranger, giving him food and clothing. Therefore love the stranger, for you were strangers in the land of Egypt. You shall fear the Lord your God; you shall serve Him, and to Him you shall hold fast, and take oaths in His name. He is your praise, and He is your God, who has done for you these great and awesome things which your eyes have seen.

<h3 style="text-align:center">1 Samuel 15:22-31</h3>

So Samuel said: "Has the Lord as great delight in burnt offerings and sacrifices, As in obeying the voice of the Lord? Behold, to obey is better than sacrifice, And to heed than the fat of rams. For rebellion is as the sin of witchcraft, And stubbornness is as iniquity and idolatry. Because you have rejected the word of the Lord, He also has rejected you from being king." Then Saul said to Samuel, "I have sinned, for I have transgressed the commandment of the Lord and your words, because I feared the people and obeyed their voice. Now therefore, please pardon my sin, and return with me, that I may worship the Lord." But Samuel said to Saul, "I will not return with you, for you have rejected the word of the Lord, and the Lord has rejected you from being king over Israel." And as Samuel turned around to go away, Saul seized the edge of his robe, and it tore. So Samuel said to him, "The Lord has torn the kingdom of Israel from you today, and has given it to a neighbor of yours, who is better than you. And also the Strength of Israel will not lie nor relent. For He is not a man, that He should relent." Then he said, "I have sinned; yet honor me now, please, before the elders of my people and before

Israel, and return with me, that I may worship the Lord your God." So Samuel turned back after Saul, and Saul worshiped the Lord.

Just a reminder that we are reading these verses to clearly maintain that God needs nothing from us.
Making it absurd to say that we could work for or earn anything from Him, let alone so great a gift as our salvation! As we finish reading through these passages, let's meditate and consider carefully our position before the all-powerful, all-righteous God who created this world and all that is in it.

Matthew 16:26
For what profit is it to a man if he gains the whole world, and loses his own soul? Or what will a man give in exchange for his soul?

Matthew 16:26 asks a powerful question! We have already discovered that God needs nothing from us. So even if we could offer Him millions of dollars or any other gift we could imagine, it would not be enough to give for our souls.

Psalm 50:9-14
I will not accept a bull from your house or goats from your folds. For every beast of the forest is mine, the cattle on a thousand hills. I know all the birds of the hills, and all that moves in the field is mine "If I were hungry, I would not tell you, for the world and its fullness are mine. Do I eat the flesh of bulls or drink the blood of goats? Offer to God a sacrifice of thanksgiving, and perform your vows to the Most High.

Psalms 50:9-14 helps us to understand why we have nothing to offer God. It is because it is all His to begin with. Again, we notice that God requires us to offer to Him the sacrifices of thanksgiving and to follow through on our promises to Him.

> *Offer to God a sacrifice of thanksgiving, and perform your vows to the Most High. (v. 14 from above)*

> *Jeremiah 9:24*
> *But let him who glories glory in this, that he understands and knows Me, that I am the LORD. exercising lovingkindness, judgment, and righteousness in the earth: for in these I delight, says the LORD.*

I love the above verse in Jeremiah. It is another reminder that we as humans really have nothing to glory about, except for our willingness to understand and know our loving and righteous Creator. It is our responsibility to seek a relationship with God! We need to seek Him through the study of His Word which is the means He has given us to come to know Him!

Luke 17:7-10 is a particularly favorite passage of mine because it is Jesus telling a story to help us understand a spiritual truth. As you read through this passage, ask yourself: Who is the servant? Who is the master?

> *Luke 17:7-10*
> *And which of you, having a servant plowing or tending sheep, will say to him when he has come in from the field, 'Come at once and sit down to eat'? But will he*

*not rather say to him, 'Prepare something for my supper,
and gird yourself and serve me till I have eaten and
drunk, and afterward you will eat and drink'? Does he
thank that servant because he did the things that were
commanded him? I think not. So likewise you, when
you have done all those things which you are
commanded, say, 'We are unprofitable servants. We
have done what was our duty to do.'*

Jesus paints a picture with this story of what our
response should to be to God, no matter what He has
asked us to do. Carefully note verse 10, Jesus makes the
point that our obedience to Him does not earn us
anything; rather, it is our Duty!

I hope these verses have helped to clearly establish that
there is no work that we could do to earn or deserve our
salvation. We can live our lives in complete sacrifice like
Mother Teresa, and yet before a righteous God we are
still in need of the blood of Jesus Christ to cleanse our
sins. Our own righteousness is as filthy rags before a
holy God, and our obedience earns us nothing.

We have seen several important concepts portrayed in
God's word. First, we are in need of being washed in the
blood of Jesus Christ to cleanse our sins. Second, our
actions are required as our duty, but they in no way earn
us anything from God.

Remember, we are trying to set a foundation on the
Words of God not on the commandments and
doctrines of men. So, let's ask our question again, "What
must I do to be saved?" Romans 6:3 is an amazing

foundational verse to help us understand how we are to be brought into contact with the blood of Jesus Christ, that we might be saved and have our sins washed away. Please, be careful to note the clear and beautiful picture that God makes for us on the way we are brought into contact with the blood of our Savior Jesus Christ that we might be saved by His blood.

We already established that "without the shedding of blood, there is no remission of sins" (Hebrews 9:22). As we will see in Romans chapter six, God has mercifully provided us a way to enter into Christ's death and be raised up with the likeness of Christ's resurrection.

The Burial that Brings Life Everlasting

Let's take time to slowly read and understand the message of Romans 6.

Romans 6:1-2
What shall we say then? Shall we continue in sin that grace may abound? Certainly not! How shall we who died to sin live any longer in it?

First, we are asked, *should we sin more so it takes more grace to cover our sin?*

We do not have to give an answer to this question because it is very firmly answered for us, *Certainly not! How shall we who died to sin live any longer in it?* So, let's answer the question.

How do we die to sin? Or asked another way, what did we do that God considers us dead to sin? Well, we don't need to answer this question either because verses 3 through 5 answer that one for us, too.

Notice that the Romans are told that they died to sin. How had they died to sin? Verse 3 tells us.

Or do you not know that as many of us as were baptized into Christ Jesus were baptized into His death?

Here it is! The answer to how the Romans had died and the answer to how they were brought into contact with Jesus Christ's blood that their sins might be washed away. God has graciously invited us into Christ's death through the waters of baptism.

Romans 6:4-5
Therefore we were buried with Him through baptism into death, that just as Christ was raised from the dead by the glory of the Father, even so we also should walk in newness of life. For if we have been united together in the likeness of His death, certainly we also shall be in the likeness of His resurrection.

So, let's ask ourselves a very important question.

What if we haven't been baptized ("united together in the likeness of his death")? The answer: then we shall not be found in the likeness of his resurrection. Right?

Romans 6:6
Knowing this, that our old man was crucified with Him, that the body of sin might be done away with, that we should no longer be slaves of sin.

If we were not baptized, then the old man and the body of sin were not destroyed. We are still serving sin.

God plainly states that when we are baptized/ immersed, we are buried with Jesus into His death. Furthermore, when we are raised out of our watery grave, we are showing forth the likeness of Jesus' resurrection. Verse eight finds us being instructed,

Romans 6:8
Now if we died with Christ, we believe that we shall
also live with him.

Would this not also mean that if we had not died with Christ (baptized with Him), we shall not live with Christ? We cannot escape the fact that if we are not baptized into Christ, we will not be raised with Christ, the old man is not put to death, and we shall not live with Christ!

Romans 6:7-8
For he who has died has been freed from sin. Now if we
died with Christ, we believe that we shall also live with
Him.

Ask yourself again, how do we die to sin?

Remember the previous verses answered this question for us. We died to sin when we entered the grave of baptism with Christ. So, if you have not entered the grave of baptism, then you did not die to sin, nor are you freed from sin.

Romans 6:8
Now if we died with Christ, we believe that we shall
also live with Him.

I know that this seems very repetitious, but God chose to be repetitious so we could clearly understand the significance of our being baptized/immersed. So, let's answer the question, "What if we have not been baptized?" Then we have not died with Christ and thus we shall not live with Christ.

Romans 6:9-11
Knowing that Christ, having been raised from the dead, dies no more. Death no longer has dominion over Him. For the death that He died, He died to sin once for all; but the life that He lives, He lives to God. Likewise you also, reckon yourselves to be dead indeed to sin, but alive to God in Christ Jesus our Lord.

How exciting! We are made "alive unto God THROUGH Jesus Christ our Lord." Wow! What an amazing visual and physical picture God has given us in Romans to help us understand both the importance and significance of our baptism. Our baptism/immersion allows us to be dead to sin and alive unto God. As we are working our way through this passage, isn't it amazing to see how many things are accomplished in our baptism/immersion?

Friend, ask yourself again, how do I die to sin so that I might be freed from sin? Romans makes this clear. It is by our baptism into Jesus Christ's death. So, to preach salvation by "grace alone" telling people to ask Jesus into their hearts and pray the sinner's prayer is giving them a false sense of salvation. Baptism is the point at which a person is brought into contact with Jesus' saving blood. They die to sin when they are buried with Christ and are raised up with Him to walk in newness of life.

Are you upset at this conclusion? Does it offend you that I am suggesting that the popular teaching of the day is not in harmony with God's Word or what Jesus and His disciples taught? Anger can be a good thing. Let it motivate you to study the Word of God diligently to "see if these things are so."

Our desire as followers of Christ should be to teach others how they might be washed of their sins and be put into Christ. There are many verses and examples throughout the New Testament that proclaim how we are to do this, and it is never to "pray the sinner's prayer" or "ask Jesus into your heart." If you doubt this, I truly beg you to read God's Word, ALL of His Word. As we turn back to our verse by verse look at Roman 6, let us try to consider what is being taught without interpreting the message with our preconceived ideas.

Romans 6:12-13
Therefore do not let sin reign in your mortal body, that you should obey it in its lusts. And do not present your members as instruments of unrighteousness to sin, but **present yourselves to God as being alive from the dead**, *and your members as instruments of righteousness to God.*

In verse thirteen, we see the passage's theme of dying to sin through our baptism/immersion and being raised up from the dead, just as Christ was raised up.
Please, ask yourself, "At what point was I raised from the dead?" You were buried in the waters of baptism and made alive by the Holy Spirit that was promised to you as you rose from the waters! Acts 2:38

Dear Friend, Romans 6:1-13 is a straightforward look at why we are baptized/immersed and the significance that is found in our being baptized. A careful consideration of this passage and simply taking what it says at face value should make it plain that baptism/immersion is an essential part of our being put into Jesus Christ.

Current doctrines being taught by many do not include embracing and teaching baptism/immersion as a necessary step to be put into Jesus Christ. That is why it is so important that we always look first to God's Word for our understanding of what He would have us to do to be saved.

Matthew 15:9
And in vain they worship Me, Teaching as doctrines the commandments of men.

2 Peter 1:20-21
Knowing this first, that no prophecy of Scripture is of any private interpretation, for prophecy never came by the will of man, but holy men of God spoke as they were moved by the Holy Spirit.

Matthew 15:9 tells us that our worship of God, however sincere, can be made vain or useless if we are following the commandments of men instead of the commandments of God. We are further told in 2 Peter 1:20-21 that God does not want us to interpret His word to our liking. He wants us to interpret His word by His word. This means that He will reveal His thoughts and commandments to us in His Word. It is our job to follow His revelation of the gospel plan for man's salvation. Let's dig in and look at all the other passages where God's word defines the importance of our baptism/immersion and what that baptism does for us! Let's take a look at verses that talk about being put into or clothed in Jesus Christ.

Galatians 3:27
For as many of you as have been baptized into Christ have put on Christ.

Galatians reaffirms that we have put on Christ when we were baptized into Him and His death, thus being brought into contact with Jesus Christ's blood and put to death with Him (Rom. 6) so that we might be raised with Him. If we put aside the teachings and commandments of men, we can see how perfectly Galatians fits with Romans. You could easily see a child being able to clearly grasp this if he was to just simply read this passage.

You might be thinking, well wait a minute, maybe this is baptism of the Holy Spirit. Let's go back to Acts 2:38 and remember that the Holy Spirit is promised after we are baptized. Gal. 3:27 is a great verse that defines what God says is accomplished by our baptism/immersion. When we are baptized into Christ we have literally put on Christ.

Titus 3:5
*Not by works of righteousness which we have done, but
according to His mercy He saved us, through the
washing of regeneration and renewing of the Holy Spirit.*

What does regeneration mean? A simple definition
would be *to make alive again.* Now that sounds familiar,
doesn't it? The *washing* of regeneration in Titus 3 is the
same *as the being made alive again* in Romans 6, when one
is baptized into Christ's death. We also see in Titus 3:5
the pattern of Acts 2:38 first baptism then the gift of the
Holy Spirit.

Please take careful note of this very present theme in
God's word. Let's be careful to not confuse *the works of
righteousness* (obeying the old law) with the obedience
God requires under the New Covenant.

Another verse that confirms God's definition of our
baptism/immersion in water is…

Colossians 2:12
*Buried with Him in baptism, in which you also were
raised with Him through faith in the working of God,
who raised Him from the dead.*

Friend, do you desire to be risen with Christ through
faith? I know that you do! Consider then how perfectly
we are told again that we must be buried in baptism with
Christ, and that it is through our baptism that we are
raised with Jesus Christ. Later in Colossians 3, we are
led through the same process of being raised with Christ

because we, **"died, and your life is hidden with Christ in God."**

Colossians 3:1-4
If then you were raised with Christ, seek those things which are above, where Christ is, sitting at the right hand of God. Set your mind on things above, not on things on the earth. For you died, and your life is hidden with Christ in God. When Christ who is our life appears, then you also will appear with Him in glory.

Please take careful note of this passage. It reads "If then you were raised with Christ." Does this statement make sense to you? When were you raised with Jesus Christ? Remember Romans chapter six. Now look at verse three. It declares that "you died and that your life is hidden with Christ." When did you die? Again, Romans chapter six clearly tells us when we died. Verse four tells us that "Christ is our life." How is Christ our life? Flip back to Romans chapter 6. Do you see the perfect puzzle piece to answer all of these questions? God's word fits together perfectly and simply, defining itself by itself.

I know this might seem redundant, but we need to see the simplicity and clarity that God's word gives us. Look at what 2 Corinthians 5:17 tells us

Therefore, if anyone is <u>in Christ</u>, he is a new creation; old things have passed away; behold, all things have become new.

We must be *In Christ* to be a new creature and for all things to become new. Notice in Ephesians 1:10 Christ will gather together in one all things *In Christ*. This leads us to ask the question, "What if you are not *In Christ?* How do I get into Christ?" The great thing is that God has answered these questions so that we do not have to wonder.

Ephesians 1:10
That in the dispensation of the fullness of the times He might gather together in one all things in Christ, both which are in heaven and which are on earth—in Him.

Notice the *In Christ!* We are constantly faced with this question, what must we do to be put *In Christ* because as we see in 2 Corinthians 5, that is how we become a new creature and make that old man of flesh die. Ephesians goes on further to tell us that God will gather together all things that are *IN CHRIST*. If someone were to ask you, "How am I put In Christ?", do you think you could answer that question according to the scriptures? Or will you ignore what God clearly states as the method by which we are put *In Christ* because it doesn't fit into the teaching and doctrines that are taught by so many? Remember the strong warnings to follow God's word only and to use all of His Word, not just the parts that seem to go along with the message that you are trying to teach. Your message after all ought to be Christ's message. They should always be interchangeable. Please take the time to read through the following verses and let them sink deep into your heart and mind for I know that you do not want to be accursed! Galatians 1:8-9

Please read these verses again.

Matthew 15:9
And in vain they worship Me, Teaching as doctrines the commandments of men.

Mark 7:7
And in vain they worship Me, Teaching as doctrines the commandments of men.

1 Timothy 4:16
Take heed to yourself and to the doctrine. Continue in them, for in doing this you will save both yourself and those who hear you.

Galatians 1:8-9
But even if we, or an angel from heaven, preach any other gospel to you than what we have preached to you, let him be accursed. As we have said before, so now I say again, if anyone preaches any other gospel to you than what you have received, let him be accursed.

Friend, please keep in mind that these are God's words and warnings, not mine. If we claim to love God, we must obey His commands.

2 John 1:9-10
Whoever transgresses and does not abide in the doctrine of Christ does not have God. He who abides in the doctrine of Christ has both the Father and the Son. If anyone comes to you and does not bring this doctrine, do not receive him into your house nor greet him.

There is not much that needs to be said about the simplicity, yet seriousness, of these verses. We must teach the doctrines of Christ; our very fellowship with God and salvation depends upon it. Are you upset that I am implying that many are not proclaiming God's message of salvation? Please, if you are, let it motivate you to honestly study through the rest of these scriptures so you can prove my error, by the Word of God!

Dear friend, I pray that you will continue to honestly ask yourself if your teachings are the same as Christ's. When you tell someone the gospel message do they respond in the same way as we see the people responded in God's Word?

The book of First John is very simple and beautiful in its proclamation of the importance of our obedience to God's commands.

1 John 5:2-3
By this we know that we love the children of God, when we love God and keep His commandments. For this is the love of God, that we keep His commandments. And His commandments are not burdensome.

1 John 2:3-6
Now by this we know that we know Him, if we keep His commandments. He who says, "I know Him," and

does not keep His commandments, is a liar, and the truth is not in him. But whoever keeps His word, truly the love of God is perfected in him. By this we know that we are in Him. He who says he abides in Him ought himself also to walk just as He walked.

Our love for God should move us to obey His doctrines and commands, and where God's commands conflict with man's doctrines, we must be found on God's side. I, for one, wish to be on God's side, I wish to stand by what He says and define His Words by His Words not my own or any other man's. I fervently pray that you will do the same.

Here are further verses that dovetail beautifully with the verses above, regarding how we are put into contact with Christ's blood, so that our sins might be washed away. Also, that we might be found *in Him.*

Philippians 3:10
That I may know Him and the power of His resurrection, and the fellowship of His sufferings, being conformed to His death.

What is the power of Jesus Christ's resurrection? The power is that we have access to the cleansing of our sins by His perfect blood. We are also told in Philippians that *"we have fellowship of His sufferings, being conformed to His death."*

My friend, ask yourself, "When did I have fellowship in His sufferings and when was I conformed to Christ's death?" Does not Romans 6, Gal. 3:27, and Col. 2:12

and many more texts explain how we know the power of His resurrection, the fellowship of His sufferings, and are conformed to His death? Can you not clearly see how perfectly God has made this picture of our death with Christ in our baptism?

Colossians 3:1
If then you were raised with Christ, seek those things which are above, where Christ is, sitting at the right hand of God.

I know that this study might seem repetitious but here it is stated that we must be raised with Christ. What have we already seen as the method by which we are risen with Christ? Please recall the passages we have read and let God's Words guide you and help you define these terms of *being put into Christ, dying with Christ,* and *being raised up with Christ,* and *being dead in Christ.*

Colossians 3:2&3
Set your mind on things above, not on things on the earth. For you died, and your life is hidden with Christ in God.

Just a reminder, in Romans Chapter 6 God defines why we are dead in Christ.

Colossians 3:4
When Christ who is our life appears, then you also will appear with Him in glory.

In this last verse, we are told that Christ is our life and because of this, we will appear with Him in Glory. We see how tremendously important it is that we be found *in Christ* if we want to appear with Him in Glory.

Ephesians 2:13-19

But now in Christ Jesus ye who sometimes were far off are made nigh by the blood of Christ. For He is our peace, who hath made both one, and hath broken down the middle wall of partition between us; Having abolished in His flesh the enmity, even the law of commandments contained in ordinances; for to make in Himself of twain one new man, so making peace; And that He might reconcile both unto God in one body by the cross, having slain the enmity thereby: And came and preached peace to you which were afar off, and to them that were nigh. For through Him we both have access by one Spirit unto the Father. Now therefore ye are no more strangers and foreigners, but fellow citizens with the saints, and of the household of God. KJV*

Consider verse 13, we are brought into Christ by His blood. We are brought in contact with His blood through baptism Rom. 6, Gal. 3:27, Col. 2:12.

1 John 5:10-13

He who believes in the Son of God has the witness in himself; he who does not believe God has made Him a liar, because he has not believed the testimony that God has given of His Son. And this is the testimony: that God has given us eternal life, and this life is in His Son. He who has the Son has life; he who does not have the Son of God does not have life. These things I have written to you who believe in the name of the Son of God, that you may know that you have eternal life, and

*that you may continue to believe in the name of the Son
of God.*

I hope that you are able to see in verse 11 that our life
is *in His Son*, and that we must have the Son in order to
have life. Those that do not have the Son do not have
life. Let us answer this important question again, "How
are we to be in the Son?" God has not left us to be
confused or to wonder at this statement. It is an open
book test; please reread Rom. 6, Gal. 3:27, Col. 2:12.

Luke 20:35-36
*But those who are counted worthy to attain that age,
and the resurrection from the dead, neither marry nor
are given in marriage; nor can they die anymore, for they
are equal to the angels and are sons of God, being sons
of the resurrection.*

It is not coincidental that we are told that those worthy
to attain to heaven will be children of the resurrection.
Why children of the resurrection? I am sure that by now
we can answer this question together and say because
we were buried with Christ in baptism that we might,
like Him, be raised to the resurrection of the dead.

Romans 5:8-9
*But God demonstrates His own love toward us, in that
while we were still sinners, Christ died for us. Much
more then, having now been justified by His blood, we
shall be saved from wrath through Him.*

Romans 5:9 tells us that we are justified by Christ's
blood, and Romans 6 tells us that we are brought into

contact with Christ's blood by being baptized into Christ's death.

Titus 3:5
Not by works of righteousness which we have done, but according to His mercy He saved us, by the washing of regeneration, and renewing of the Holy Spirit.

In Titus, we find that the *washing of regeneration* or baptism is not considered by God a work. It is an act of obedience to what He has commanded in His word. I would ask you to please recall that there is nothing that we could give or do that would earn us our salvation.

Please, friend, if you were not clear on that, go back and reread what God's Word has said on the matter.

1 Peter 3:20-21
who formerly were disobedient, when once the Divine long-suffering waited in the days of Noah, while the ark was being prepared, in which a few, that is, eight souls, were saved through water. There is also an antitype which now saves us—baptism (not the removal of the filth of the flesh, but the answer of a good conscience toward God), through the resurrection of Jesus Christ.

Titus 3:5 and 1 Peter 3:20-21 speak with unity and oneness on the washing that is required to put us into Christ Jesus so that our sins might be washed away. They both state that we are brought in contact with Christ's death and His blood when we are buried with Him into baptism. If we believe and are not yet baptized, we do not have the promise of Rom. 6 and

Gal. 3:27, that we will rise with Christ. If we are not washed, our sins have not been wiped away or forgiven.

I know that this still might be hard to accept since so many of man's doctrines teach that we are saved by grace alone, to pray the sinner's prayer and ask Jesus into your heart, and you will be saved. I must ask you, do the above verses teach that? I hope that you can answer, **NO** to that question, or at least after examining these verses, that you seriously have your doubts.

Whatever the case may be, let us move on to the book of Acts and its record of the early church. You will see example after example of people being saved and put into Christ in the same manner as the previous verses have mentioned. The early Christians left us an example to follow. When the gospel message is heard what is the response we repeatedly see recorded in God's Word?

Stories of Salvation

The following passages show the pattern that the Bible gives us for salvation. We see the scriptural accounts of people being saved are the same throughout the book of Acts. As an individual hears the gospel and is pricked to the heart and believes the message of salvation, they repent of their sins, confess Jesus as Christ, and are baptized into Jesus Christ's death, so they might have their sins washed away, and be put into Christ (Rom. 6, Col. 3:1-4, Gal. 3:27, Col. 2:12).

Acts 16:25-40

But at midnight Paul and Silas were praying and singing hymns to God, and the prisoners were listening to them. Suddenly there was a great earthquake, so that the foundations of the prison were shaken; and immediately all the doors were opened and everyone's chains were loosed. And the keeper of the prison, awaking from sleep and seeing the prison doors open, supposing the prisoners had fled, drew his sword and was about to kill himself.

But Paul called with a loud voice, saying, "Do yourself no harm, for we are all here." Then he called for a light, ran in, and fell down trembling before Paul and Silas. And he brought them out and said, "Sirs, what must I do to be saved?" So they said, "Believe on the Lord Jesus Christ, and you will be saved, you and your household." Then they spoke the word of the Lord to him and to all who were in his house. And he took them the same hour of the night and washed their stripes.

And immediately he and all his family were baptized. Now when he had brought them into his house, he set food before them; and he rejoiced, having believed in God with all his household. And when it was day, the magistrates sent the officers, saying, "Let those men go." So the keeper of the prison reported these words to Paul, saying, "The magistrates have sent to let you go. Now therefore depart, and go in peace." But Paul said to them, "They have beaten us openly, uncondemned Romans, and have thrown us into prison. And now do they put us out secretly? No indeed! Let them come themselves and get us out." And the officers told these words to the magistrates, and they were afraid when they heard that they were Romans.

Then they came and pleaded with them and brought them out, and asked them to depart from the city. So they went out of the prison and entered the house of Lydia; and when they had seen the brethren, they encouraged them and departed.

The time is midnight or later, and yet they went that same hour to be baptized. Baptism always immediately follows conviction and belief (Acts 16:25-40).

Let's consider more examples of this biblical pattern for salvation (belief, repentance, confession, being baptized, and walking in love and obedience to Christ).
The books of James and 1 John both show the importance of belief, obedience, and actions. I would strongly encourage you to read both books right now so that you might see for yourself the harmony in God's word. These two books show belief being manifested by

one's obedience. For example in 1 John, God without apology tells us that if we do not have love in our hearts for others, we do not have a relationship with God or love for Him! Demonstrating that our actions should openly declare our beliefs!

Let's get back to the examples of people hearing the gospel plan for man's salvation and their responses to that message.

Lydia believed and was baptized. Note that she heard the message as spoken by the apostles, she believed what they said, and was immediately baptized.

Acts 16:11-15

Therefore, sailing from Troas, we ran a straight course to Samothrace, and the next day came to Neapolis, and from there to Philippi, which is the foremost city of that part of Macedonia, a colony. And we were staying in that city for some days. And on the Sabbath day we went out of the city to the riverside, where prayer was customarily made; and we sat down and spoke to the women who met there. Now a certain woman named Lydia heard us. She was a seller of purple from the city of Thyatira, who worshiped God. The Lord opened her heart to heed the things spoken by Paul. And when she and her household were baptized, she begged us, saying, "If you have judged me to be faithful to the Lord, come to my house and stay." So she persuaded us.

Crispus and many of the Corinthians upon hearing the words of life spoken by the apostles believed what they heard and were baptized.

Acts 18:8
Then Crispus, the ruler of the synagogue, believed on the Lord with all his household. And many of the Corinthians, hearing, believed and were baptized.

Again, please note the wealth of the examples that the Lord saw fit to include in His word of people being saved, so we could be confident and without doubt as to what we must do. Acts chapter eight gives us several more examples of the results of someone hearing the gospel plan for man's salvation preached. I think that you will agree with me that it looks rather familiar to all the rest of the examples. The people heard, believed, confessed and were baptized.

Acts 8:12-13
But when they believed Philip as he preached the things concerning the kingdom of God and the name of Jesus Christ, both men and women were baptized. Then Simon himself also believed; and when he was baptized he continued with Philip, and was amazed, seeing the and miracles signs which were done.

H. Roye

If You Preached the Gospel Plan of Salvation to Someone

If someone were to ask you, "What must I do to be saved?" what would your response be?

Specifically, what would you teach them as to the gospel's plan for man's salvation? Please, take some time to really answer this question!

Now, let's pretend that the person you were speaking to was convicted and wanted to follow what you had just taught them, what would they say to you?
Again, play this scenario out in your mind!

Based upon what you had just taught them, what would their response be to you?

Would they say something like, "I want to ask Jesus into my heart", or "Will you pray the sinner's prayer with me?" Would you agree that this is the response that you would hear? (Write it down.)

I would like you to look again at what the response was to the apostle's teaching the gospels plan for man's salvation. You will see that there is a big difference between the response given to the apostles and the response that you would have expected to your own gospel message.

67

Acts 8:35-39

Then Philip opened his mouth, and beginning at this Scripture, preached Jesus to him. Now as they went down the road, they came to some water. And the eunuch said, "See, here is water. What hinders me from being baptized?" Then Philip said, "If you believe with all your heart, you may." And he answered and said, "I believe that Jesus Christ is the Son of God." So he commanded the chariot to stand still. And both Philip and the eunuch went down into the water, and he baptized him. Now when they came up out of the water, the Spirit of the Lord caught Philip away, so that the eunuch saw him no more; and he went on his way rejoicing.

Friend, please notice Philip preaches Jesus Christ to the eunuch and after the eunuch has heard the message, they happen to be passing by some water and he says, *"What hinders me from being baptized?"* Please consider with me what Philip must have preached to him for this to be his response.

We can logically deduce, based on the eunuch's response to Philip's message, exactly what Philip proclaimed to the eunuch as the gospel's plan for man's salvation. The logical answer is the same message that was proclaimed by the apostles in Acts 2:37-38.

Acts 2:37-38

Now when they heard this, they were cut to the heart, and said to Peter and to the rest of the apostles, "Men and brethren, what shall we do?" Then Peter said to them, "Repent, and let every one of you be baptized in

> *the name of Jesus Christ for the remission of sins, and you shall receive the gift of the Holy Spirit."*

It is obvious and logical that Philip preached the same message to the eunuch that Peter and the rest of the apostles preached to the multitude: the message of belief in Jesus Christ, repentance of sins, confession of Jesus, and baptism. As we read the book of Acts, this is always the pattern that those wishing to be born again followed.

I want to take a minute here to add a little side note about this verse. Several times in studying the scriptures with others, I have been told that the *for* in Acts 2:38 is more accurately translated as *because of.* Making the scripture read,

> *Then Peter said to them, "Repent, and let every one of you be baptized in the name of Jesus Christ <u>because of</u> the remission of sins; and you shall receive the gift of the Holy Spirit.*

Let's address that right now. The word *for* is translated many times in the Bible and it is NEVER translated as *because of.* Yet in this one verse, men try to change its meaning to fit God's word into their personal beliefs or doctrines. Study this one out and you will find the shocking truth that this verse has been distorted to fit into man's doctrines. The interesting point here is that if we just read it for what it says,

...be baptized every one of you in the name of Jesus Christ for the remission of sins, and ye shall receive the gift of the Holy Spirit.

the verse is perfectly consistent with the rest of the Word of God and the conversion stories throughout the book of Acts. Let's not be guilty of trying to change God's Word, especially in a deceptive way to mislead others, as Satan did Eve in the Garden of Eden!

The Three-day Long "Sinner's Prayer" That Did Not Save

Dear Friend, did you know that the Bible gives an example of a fervent three-day-long sinner's prayer that was accompanied by both steadfast belief and fasting, and yet it **did *not* save or remit the sinner's sins**? Hard to believe? I know, especially in light of mainstream Christianity teaching that the sinner's prayer and asking Jesus into your heart, is the process by which we are saved and have our sins removed. But let us call to mind again that we are to follow hard after God and His Word and not the doctrines and commandments of men.

Matthew 15:9; Mark 7:7
And in vain they worship Me,
Teaching as doctrine the commandments of men.

Are you ready? Then let's dig deep into God's Word and read about the three-day-long sinner's prayer that was unable to save and cleanse the sinner of his sins.

Acts 9:1-19
Then Saul, still breathing threats and murder against the disciples of the Lord, went to the high priest and asked letters from him to the synagogues of Damascus, so that if he found any who were of the Way, whether men or women, he might bring them bound to Jerusalem.

*As he journeyed he came near Damascus, and suddenly
a light shone around him from heaven. Then he fell to
the ground, and heard a voice saying to him, "Saul,
Saul, why are you persecuting Me?" And he said,
"Who are You, Lord?" Then the Lord said, "I am
Jesus, whom you are persecuting. It is hard for you to
kick against the goads." So he, trembling and
astonished, said, "Lord, what do You want me to do?"
Then the Lord said to him, "Arise and go into the city,
and you will be told what you must do." And the men
who journeyed with him stood speechless, hearing a voice
but seeing no one.*

*Then Saul arose from the ground, and when his
eyes were opened he saw no one. But they led him by
the hand and brought him into Damascus. And he
was three days without sight, and neither ate nor drank.
Now there was a certain disciple at Damascus named
Ananias; and to him the Lord said in a vision,
"Ananias." And he said, "Here I am, Lord." So the
Lord said to him, "Arise and go to the street called
Straight, and inquire at the house of Judas for one called
Saul of Tarsus, for behold, he is praying. And in a
vision he has seen a man named Ananias coming in
and putting his hand on him, so that he might receive
his sight." Then Ananias answered, "Lord, I have
heard from many about this man, how much harm he
has done to Your saints in Jerusalem. And here he has
authority from the chief priests to bind all who call on
Your name." But the Lord said to him, "Go, for he is
a chosen vessel of Mine to bear My name before
Gentiles, kings, and the children of Israel. For I will
show him how many things he must suffer for My*

name's sake." And Ananias went his way and entered the house; and laying his hands on him he said, "Brother Saul, the Lord Jesus, who appeared to you on the road as you came, has sent me that you may receive your sight and be filled with the Holy Spirit." Immediately there fell from his eyes something like scales, and he received his sight at once; and he arose and was baptized. So when he had received food, he was strengthened. Then Saul spent some days with the disciples at Damascus.

I know that you have probably read the story of Paul's conversion a hundred times but let's look at it together carefully. Consider who Saul is at this time in his life, someone who is an expert in the Jewish culture and way of life. Also, he knew of Jesus and His followers and was trying to single-handedly eradicate them. As he is traveling to Damascus to do just that, Jesus appears to him in a vision and Saul has a conversation with Jesus Christ! So I will ask you, at what point during the story of Paul's conversion would you say that he was saved, put into Christ Jesus and had his sins washed away?

Please, really give this question some serious thought! To be consistent with mainstream teachings, you would probably have to answer that Saul was saved at the point of belief, which of course is when he met, spoke to, and saw Jesus Christ while still on the road to Damascus.

Is that correct? Would that not be the most consistent answer to the faith only belief, that one is saved at the point of belief in Jesus Christ?

Let's look at Paul's second account where he is retelling how he came to believe in Christ Jesus as his Lord and Savior. Notice that we are not left to guess or make assumptions as to the exact moment in which Paul was saved (put into Christ and had his sins washed away). He is quite direct on this point and leaves no room for us to misunderstand at what point his sins were washed away. Let's read his account with an open mind and a true desire to see the truth and not try to fit our preconceived doctrinal ideas into God's word.

Acts 22:1-16

*"Brethren and fathers, hear my defense before you now."
And when they heard that he spoke to them in the
Hebrew language, they kept all the more silent.
Then he said: "I am indeed a Jew, born in Tarsus of
Cilicia, but brought up in this city at the feet of
Gamaliel, taught according to the strictness of our
fathers' law, and was zealous toward God as you all
are today. I persecuted this Way to the death, binding
and delivering into prisons both men and women, as also
the high priest bears me witness, and all the council of
the elders, from whom I also received letters to the
brethren, and went to Damascus to bring in chains even
those who were there to Jerusalem to be punished. Now
it happened, as I journeyed and came near Damascus
at about noon, suddenly a great light from heaven shone
around me. And I fell to the ground and heard a voice
saying to me, 'Saul, Saul, why are you persecuting Me?'
So I answered, 'Who are You, Lord?' And He said to
me, 'I am Jesus of Nazareth, whom you are
persecuting.' And those who were with me indeed saw
the light and were afraid, but they did not hear the voice*

of Him who spoke to me. So I said, 'What shall I do, Lord?' And the Lord said to me, 'Arise and go into Damascus, and there you will be told all things which are appointed for you to do.' And since I could not see for the glory of that light, being led by the hand of those who were with me, I came into Damascus. Then a certain Ananias, a devout man according to the law, having a good testimony with all the Jews who dwelt there, came to me; and he stood and said to me, 'Brother Saul, receive your sight.' And at that same hour I looked up at him. Then he said, 'The God of our fathers has chosen you that you should know His will, and see the Just One, and hear the voice of His mouth. For you will be His witness to all men of what you have seen and heard. And now why are you waiting? Arise and be baptized, and wash away your sins, calling on the name of the Lord.'"

As you carefully read through the passage above, I want you to consider several things.

First, what do you think Paul was saying to God as he fervently prayed and fasted for three long days? (Write it down.)

If we could have heard what he said, I bet on a scale of most sincere, fervent prayers of forgiveness and asking the Lord into one's life, this prayer by Paul could have taken top three if not number one.

We clearly see in Paul's conversion that he believed and accompanied that belief with a sincere sinner's prayer and fasting for three days, and yet we can see by verse

16 that he was not saved (put into Christ nor had his sins been washed away).

If you want to contend that someone is saved (put into Christ and their sins washed) at the point of belief, then Paul should have been saved on the road to Damascus where he came face to face with Jesus Christ.

But as you can clearly see from the above passage, note verse 16, this is not the case.

It is also clearly NOT the case that his fervent sinner's prayer washed his sins away or put him into Christ.
So, what do we see?

Well, notice after all of Paul's prayers, his fasting, and belief in Jesus Christ, Ananias comes to him and says,

> *And now why are you waiting? Arise and be baptized, and wash away your sins, calling on the name of the Lord. (Acts 22:16)*

This verse is not cryptic or hard to understand.
It clearly shows that Paul had not been put into Christ (saved or his sins washed away), and further, that he needed to be baptized to accomplish the washing away of his sins.

Friend, I hope that you can see how perfectly Paul's conversion fits with the other conversions in the book of Acts and the other verses we just read which teach that we are put into Christ (saved and our sins washed) when we are buried with Christ in water baptism.

Paul's conversion shows us that it is at the point of water baptism that our sins are washed away and that we are put into Jesus Christ. Yet, people are taught that if they just believe, ask Jesus into their heart, and pray the sinner's prayer, their sins are washed away and they are put into Jesus Christ.

In telling people they are saved when they believe, we are standing in opposition to what God's Word directly declares to us as truth and the way to be put into Christ or washed in the blood of Christ (Rom. 6; Col. 3; Gal. 3:27; Col. 2:12).

Will you object on the grounds that the baptism is not water baptism, but really baptism of the Holy Spirit? I hope that you can clearly see from the context of these passages that claiming baptism of the Holy Spirit would not make sense, since all the language clearly points to water baptism. Also, the gift of the Holy Spirit was not promised until after the point of water baptism; please read Acts 2:38 again.

> *Then Peter said unto them, "Repent, and let every one of you be baptized in the name of Jesus Christ for the remission of sins; and you shall receive the gift of the Holy Spirit."*

The Bible further emphasizes the significance of water baptism/immersion in the following scripture:

Romans 8:5-11

For those who live according to the flesh set their minds on the things of the flesh, but those who live according to the Spirit, the things of the Spirit. For to be carnally minded is death, but to be spiritually minded is life and peace. Because the carnal mind is enmity against God; for it is not subject to the law of God, nor indeed can be. So then, those who are in the flesh cannot please God. But you are not in the flesh but in the Spirit, if indeed the Spirit of God dwells in you. <u>Now if anyone does not have the Spirit of Christ, he is not His</u>. And if Christ is in you, the body is dead because of sin, but the Spirit is life because of righteousness. But if the Spirit of Him who raised Jesus from the dead dwells in you, He who raised Christ from the dead will also give life to your mortal bodies through His Spirit who dwells in you.

Especially note verses 8-11, and as you read through this passage, carefully consider that the Bible clearly states (Acts 2:38) that we are not promised the gift of the Holy Spirit until after the point of water baptism/immersion. So just to be very clear, if you have not been baptized, then you do not have the Holy Spirit living in you. The above passage in Romans is very clear and simple in its declaration that if you do not have the Holy Spirit, then you are NOT His. The passage further goes on to explicitly state that we are only given life through the Spirit that dwells in us. So, consider and ask yourself, "How important is water baptism/immersion?"

Romans states that it is the difference between being dead and being alive! Being God's enemy or being found in Him!

When you stand before a righteous God someday, you will not want to stand before Him as His enemy. You will want to be found *in Him*, washed of your sins and covered in the shed blood of our Lord and Savior Jesus Christ.

We Must Be Baptized
into Jesus Christ's Death!

Now, turn with me to an actual account of believers not receiving the Holy Ghost because they were not baptized/immersed into Jesus Christ's death.

Acts 19:2-7
He said to them, "Did you receive the Holy Spirit when you believed?" So they said to him, "We have not so much as heard whether there is a Holy Spirit." And he said to them, "Into what then were you baptized?" So they said, "Into John's baptism." Then Paul said, "John indeed baptized with a baptism of repentance, saying to the people that they should believe on Him who would come after him, that is, on Christ Jesus." When they heard this, they were baptized in the name of the Lord Jesus. And when Paul had laid hands on them, the Holy Spirit came upon them, and they spoke with tongues and prophesied. Now the men were about twelve in all.

Please, notice that *belief* and the act of obedience being baptized/immersed are presented as one inseparable step that is taken before we receive the Gift of the Holy Spirit.

Let's start at verse 2 where Paul asks them, "Did you receive the Holy Spirit when you believed?" To which the <u>believers</u> respond, "We didn't even know there was a Holy Spirit." Now this is the important point. Paul does not ask, "Didn't you ask Jesus into your hearts?"

Or "Didn't you say the sinner's prayer?"
or even,
"You are saved by belief and faith only, so did you not really believe or maybe you just don't have enough faith?"
No, Paul's immediate response is, *"Into what then were you baptized?"*

By this response, Paul is ending any argument that could be made as to the point at which the believer receives the Holy Spirit.

Because again, as Acts 2:38 states, *believers* must repent and be baptized and then they are promised the gift of the Holy Spirit. Now you might try to argue that, "Well, yes, they were baptized, but then it says that the Holy Spirit came upon them when Paul laid his hands on them." Keep in mind that if they could have received the Holy Spirit simply from Paul laying his hands on them, Paul would not have asked them about which baptism they were baptized with. He would have simply laid his hands on them! And why bother baptizing them again if he could have just laid his hands on them?

Paul did not do this, because he understood that they must be put into contact with Jesus Christ's blood through water baptism/immersion just as Romans 6, Col.2:12, Acts 2:38, 1 Peter 3:21 and Gal.3:27 tell us.

Maybe There Are Two Baptisms?

Will you object on the grounds that the baptism is not water baptism but really baptism of the Holy Spirit? I hope that you can clearly see from these passages that claiming baptism of the Holy Spirit would not make sense, since all the language clearly points to water baptism. Also, the gift of the Holy Spirit was not promised until after the point of water baptism; please reread Acts 2:38.

> *Then Peter said to them, "Repent, and let every one of you be baptized in the name of Jesus Christ for the remission of sins; and you shall receive the gift of the Holy Spirit."*

And just in case you might think, well then there must be two baptisms and we get to pick and choose when the scripture means water baptism versus baptism of the Holy Spirit. God's word states that there is *one baptism*.

> *Ephesians 4:4-6*
> *There is one body and one Spirit, just as you were called in one hope of your calling; one Lord, one faith, one baptism; one God and Father of all, who is above all, and through all, and in you all.*

Let's Define the Greek Word *Baptism*

It is also important to remember that the word *baptism* is a Greek word that the translators did not translate into English; they transliterated it. Wow, what does that mean?

It simply means that instead of translating the word baptism into English, they simply carried it over into the text in its Greek form. The Greek word *baptism* is equivalent to the English word *immersion*.

Why am I mentioning this to you? Because the Greek word baptism literally means *immersion*!

It is very unfortunate that our translations use the Greek word baptism rather than the English word immerse. Could you not agree that a lot of confusion would be wiped away if we knew that the Greek word baptism actually means to immerse?

Can you think of some mistakes that would not be made? For example, sprinkling or pouring water over people and calling that immersion would not make sense or be practiced by those trying to obey God's command to be immersed!

I would also like you to call to mind again Romans 6, where baptism/immersion is symbolizing going into the grave as our Lord Jesus Christ did. Immersion is a perfect symbolic way to do that; pouring and sprinkling are not.

Our Lord Commanded Water Baptism

Let's not forget that water baptism was a direct command given by Jesus Christ while He was on earth.

Matthew 28:18-20
And Jesus came and spoke to them, saying, "All authority has been given to Me in heaven and on earth. Go therefore and make disciples of all the nations, baptizing (immersing) them in the name of the Father and of the Son and of the Holy Spirit, teaching them to observe all things that I have commanded you; and lo, I am with you always, even to the end of the age." Amen.

Mark 16:16
He who believes and is baptized (immersed) will be saved; but he who does not believe will be condemned.

Who owns your allegiance?

Are we saved by grace ALONE?

Do we just need to say the sinner's prayer and ask Jesus into our hearts?

Is that what the Word of God teaches?

Again, remember that our only allegiance should be to God and His Word, not to any man or his doctrines. And when we see that the doctrines of man are not teaching what Jesus and His apostles taught, our duty is to be found on God's side no matter who is on the other side!

"If I profess, with the loudest voice and the clearest exposition, every portion of the truth of God except precisely that little point which the world and the devil are at that moment attacking, I am not confessing Christ, however boldly I may be professing Christianity."

"Where the battle rages, the loyalty of the soldier is proved; and to be steady on all the battle-field besides is mere flight and disgrace to him if he flinches at that one point." ~ Martin Luther

---

You have a few objections…

I know that you are probably thinking of several objections that you would like to present to me that you believe would contradict the role that baptism plays.

Things like, the thief on the cross, Cornelius, and that Mark 16:16 doesn't say…

Mark 16:16

*He who believes and is baptized will be saved; but he who does not believe **"and is not baptized"** will be condemned* (This is written wrong as an example).

You would also probably like to tell me a little story that goes something like this, "A man believes the message of salvation and is on his way to be baptized and he is killed in a car accident on the way; is he saved?"

Okay, my friend, I will address those questions, so if you can't wait, then skip ahead to the answers to your questions. (But...What About...? Pg. 148) But promise me that you will come back to this point so that you are able to see and absorb all the scriptures that pertain to our salvation.

What if I was baptized with the wrong understanding?

What should you do if you have been baptized, however, your understanding as to baptism's purpose was wrong? When you were baptized you believed that its purpose was an outward sign of an inward grace or anything other than its real purpose, to forgive your sin and put you into Christ. Well, would you believe it? God has provided us with an example of a misunderstanding of the way of salvation and what we ought to do if we find ourselves in this situation. Let's read,

Acts 19:2-7

He said to them, "Did you receive the Holy Spirit when you believed?" So they said to him, "We have not so much as heard whether there is a Holy Spirit." And he said to them, "Into what then were you baptized?" So they said, "Into John's baptism." Then Paul said, "John indeed baptized with the baptism of repentance, saying to the people, that they should believe on him who would come after him, that is, on Christ Jesus." When they heard this, they were baptized in the name of the Lord Jesus. And when Paul had laid his hands on them, the Holy Spirit came on them; and they spoke with tongues and prophesied. Now the men were about twelve in all."

Why had these individuals not received the Holy Spirit? Well, what does Acts 2:38 tell us about when we receive the Holy Spirit?

Acts 2:38

Then Peter said to them, "Repent, and let every one of you be baptized in the name of Jesus Christ for the remission of sins; and you shall receive the gift of the Holy Spirit."

Here we go: It says we believe, repent and are baptized, *then* we are promised the Holy Spirit. The reason these individuals in Acts 19:2-7 hadn't received the Holy Spirit yet is because they hadn't been baptized into Jesus Christ's death.

So, we see that they were baptized again because we need to be baptized into Christ so that we can put on

Christ and receive the promise of the Holy Spirit (Rom. 6, Col. 3, Gal. 3:27, Col. 2:12).

More food for thought!

The word of God is so full of examples that serve to show that we have a part to play in our own salvation, and if by faith we obey and do our part, God gives us blessings and gifts that we could never earn or deserve. Let's read these great examples and put some time into considering the pattern that is put forth by them.

John 9:7-11

And He said to him, "Go, wash in the pool of Siloam" (which is translated, Sent.) So he went and washed, and came back seeing. Therefore the neighbors and those who previously had seen that he was blind, said, "Is not this he who sat and begged?" Some said, "This is he." Others said, "He is like him." He said, "I am he." Therefore said they to him, "How were your eyes opened?" He answered and said, "A man called Jesus made clay and anointed mine eyes and   said to me, 'Go to the pool of Siloam, and wash.' So I went and washed, and I received sight."

Did the blind man earn or deserve his sight because he went and washed? Of course not!

Likewise, we didn't earn our salvation because we washed in the waters of baptism. In both cases, something was accomplished that we could not have accomplished for ourselves, no matter how much money we had or what we did or sacrificed. The gift of sight to the blind man and, unfathomably more precious, the salvation from our sins is out of our reach, no matter what we were to do.

The story of Naaman is another wonderful example, especially verse 13, because many people are willing to believe, repent, and confess, and yet they stumble at baptism. Naaman's servant's wisdom and words are so timeless and resounding with truth for everyone, for all time.

2 Kings 5:13

And his servants came near and spoke to him, and said, "My father, if the prophet had told you to do something great, would you not have done it? How much more then, when he says to you, 'Wash, and be clean'?"

Another interesting point here is that Naaman believed that Elisha could heal him and had faith enough to travel to see him. However, this belief would have profited him nothing if he had not obeyed and washed in the Jordan. He was cleansed at the point of washing and not belief. (Goes along rather nicely with the book of James, *"Faith without works is dead."*) A parallel to Naaman's cleansing is the cleansing of our sins in the watery grave of baptism. We are cleansed at the point of washing, not belief (Acts 2:38, Acts 22:16, 1 Peter 3:21).

We will read the story together and see the beauty of God's relationship with man, and how it has been consistent from Genesis to Revelation. Man obeys

God's commands and God accomplishes a miraculous work that man could never have attained on his own.

2 Kings 5:1-19

Now Naaman, commander of the army of the king of Syria, was a great and honorable man in the eyes of his master, because by him the Lord had given victory to Syria. He was also a mighty man of valor, but a leper. And the Syrians had gone out on raids, and had brought back captive a young girl from the land of Israel. She waited on Naaman's wife. Then she said to her mistress, "If only my master were with the prophet who is in Samaria! For he would heal him of his leprosy." And Naaman went in and told his master, saying, "Thus and thus said the girl who is from the land of Israel." Then the king of Syria said, "Go now, and I will send a letter to the king of Israel." So he departed and took with him ten talents of silver, six thousand shekels of gold, and ten changes of clothing. Then he brought the letter to the king of Israel, which said,

> *Now be advised, when this letter comes to you, that I have sent Naaman my servant to you, that you may heal him of his leprosy.*

And it happened, when the king of Israel read the letter, that he tore his clothes and said, "Am I God, to kill and make alive, that this man sends a man to me to heal him of his leprosy? Therefore please consider, and see how he seeks a quarrel with me." So it was, when Elisha the man of God heard that the king of Israel had torn his clothes, that he sent to the king, saying, "Why have you torn your clothes? Please let him come to me, and he shall know that there is a prophet in

Israel." Then Naaman went with his horses and chariot, and he stood at the door of Elisha's house. And Elisha sent a messenger to him, saying, "Go and wash in the Jordan seven times, and your flesh shall be clean." But Naaman became furious, and went away and said, "Indeed, I said to myself, 'He will surely come out to me, and stand and call on the name of the Lord his God, and wave his hand over the place, and heal the leprosy.' Are not the Abanah and the Pharpar, the rivers of Damascus, better than all the waters of Israel? Could I not wash in them and be clean?" So he turned and went away in rage. And his servants came near and spoke to him, and said, "My father, if the prophet had told you to do something great, would you not have done it? How much more then, when he says to you, 'Wash, and be clean'?" So he went down and dipped seven times in the Jordan, according to the saying of the man of God; and his flesh was restored like the flesh of a little child, and he was clean. And he returned to the man of God, he and his aides, and came and stood before him: and he said, "Indeed, now I know that there is no God in all the earth, except in Israel; now therefore, please take a gift from your servant." But he said, "As the LORD lives, before whom I stand, I will receive nothing." And he urged him to take it, but he refused. So Naaman said, "Then, if not, please let your servant be given two mule-loads of earth; for your servant will no longer offer either burnt offerings or sacrifice to other gods, but to the LORD. Yet in this thing may the LORD pardon your servant: when my master goes into the temple of Rimmon to worship there, and he leans on my hand, and I bow down in the temple of Rimmon — when I bow down in the temple of Rimmon, may the LORD please pardon your servant in this thing." Then he said to him, "Go in peace." So he departed from him a short distance."

Let's take special note of verse fifteen, Naaman obeyed and washed in the Jordan as he was told. Yet you do not see him being so foolish as to say, "I healed myself...I earned my salvation from leprosy!" He does the complete opposite, let's read, *"and he said, 'Indeed, now I know that there is no God in all the earth, except in Israel.'"* (vs. 15).

Naaman obeyed and actively went and washed himself, yet he never thought for one second that his action did the miracle. He knew and acknowledged that it was God who saved him from his leprosy.

One more interesting passage in the Old Testament in which we can see the parallel that *faith alone* does not save, is when God sent serpents among the people and they were told to look upon the serpent that Moses erected in order to be healed from a serpent bite (Numbers 21:8-9).

As you read this passage, I ask you to be honest with yourself and true to the passage that you are reading. Ask yourself, "If someone had faith that looking upon the serpent would heal them, yet refused to go look upon the serpent, would their faith save them?"

I hope that, like in the passage of the blind man, and of Naaman, you can clearly see that it is an *active faith* that leads to obedience to God's commands that saves.

The full picture as presented by the Word of God

We have seen that we are saved by the blood of Jesus Christ and that we are brought into contact with that blood in the waters of baptism. God's word has clearly shown us that baptism forgives our sin and puts us into Jesus Christ. So the blood of Jesus Christ saves us. The Word of God teaches that baptism along with twenty or so other actions are all part of salvation. It is important that you know and understand this full picture of ALL the things that work together for the salvation of mankind. A look at the following passages will help you to see the full picture of what God says works together for our salvation.

God has said that the sum of His Word is truth, so of course baptism is only one ingredient in our salvation. And just as you do not have chocolate chip cookies if you just have chocolate chips, salvation is not found in Baptism, Grace, Repentance, Confession, or a Faithful life alone. God's recipe for salvation is found in the sum of all that He has revealed to us in His Word.

Don't worry! I did not forget about your objections (the thief on the cross, Cornelius, etc…) as to why baptism could not be necessary, and we will get to those presently. But first you must catch a glimpse of the many things that God declares to work out our salvation. Why is this so important? Because *the sum of God's word is truth,* so everything that God has declared saves us is of equal value to God and must be equally valued and taught by us as well.

We have no authority to select our favorites and leave out the rest of what God has declared for salvation.

Matthew 4:4
But He answered and said, "It is written, 'Man shall not live by bread alone, but by every word that proceeds from the mouth of God.'"

Remember we are to live by **every word of God,** and nothing is accomplished by trying to make God's Word contradict itself by trying to pit one scripture against another. The only thing accomplished by this is rebellion to God's written commands. As we begin a little journey through the scriptures examining the actions necessary for our salvation, be sure to read the following scriptures with an open heart that loves truth. Examine the scriptures and see for yourself if these things are so. We all have our prejudices and our preconceived ideas so it is important to just read what is written and as a child would accept the truths as God has revealed them to us in His Word.

PART 2

The Bible Tells Us that
Over 20 Different Things Save Us

As we already studied, God's grace, blood, and baptism into Jesus Christ's death saves us. Now let's allow God's word to add a few more to our list.

Grace Saves Us

> *Acts 15:11*
> *But we believe that through the grace of the Lord Jesus Christ we shall be saved in the same manner as they.*

> *Romans 3:24*
> *Being justified freely by his grace through the redemption that is in Christ Jesus.*

> *Ephesians 2:8*
> *For by grace you have been saved through faith, and that not of yourselves; it is the gift of God, not of works, lest anyone should boast.*

I think that it is repetitious, but extremely important, that I mention again that the Bible teaches that grace saves us, but the phrases, *GRACE ALONE, AND ONLY GRACE* are additions of men and not found in the Bible. Like in the Garden of Eden, the serpent changed God's word by ONE word. This distorted God's message. The results of changing God's word by even one little word like ALONE or ONLY also shows disrespect for God's message. The end result in the garden was physical death and separation from God. Let's be very careful that we add nothing to God's word.

Proverbs 30:6
Do not add to His words,
Lest He rebuke you, and you be found a liar.

Pretty strong warning, would you not agree, my friend?

Faith Saves Us

Hebrews 11:6
But without faith it is impossible to please Him, for he who comes to God must believe that He is, and that He is a rewarder of those who diligently seek Him.

Hebrews 10:39
But we are not of those who draw back to perdition, but of those who believe to the saving of the soul.

2 Timothy 1:12
For this reason I also suffer these things; nevertheless I am not ashamed, for I know whom I have believed and am persuaded that He is able to keep what I have committed to Him until that Day.

Romans 5:1-2
Therefore, having been justified by faith, we have peace with God through our Lord Jesus Christ, through whom also we have access by faith into this grace in which we stand, and rejoice in hope of the glory of God.

Now my friend, I do not want you to miss this last verse on faith. Please read it carefully. James 2:24 is the only time that the Bible uses the phrase *"FAITH ONLY"* and I believe that you will again see a one-word deception of Satan. This time, however, Satan **removed** just one little word because the verse says, "NOT by faith only." So you see, my friend, the word of God proclaims boldly that we are NOT saved by FAITH ONLY, GRACE ONLY, OR GRACE ALONE.

James 2:24
You see then that a man is justified by works, and not by faith only.

Jesus' Blood Saves Us

1 John 1:7
But if we walk in the light, as He is in the light, we have fellowship one with another, and the blood of Jesus Christ His Son cleanses us from all sin.

Romans 5:9
Much more then, having now been justified by His blood, we shall be saved from wrath through Him.

Ephesians 1:7
In Him we have redemption through His blood, the forgiveness of sins, according to the riches of His grace.

Baptism in Water Saves Us

1 Peter 3:20-21

Who formerly were disobedient, when once the Divine longsuffering waited in the days of Noah, while the ark was being prepared, in which a few, that is, eight souls, were saved through water. There is also an antitype which now saves us — baptism (not for the removal of the filth of the flesh, but the answer of a good conscience toward God), through the resurrection of Jesus Christ.

Acts 22:16

And now why are you waiting? Arise and be baptized, and wash away your sins, calling on the name of the Lord.

Colossians 2:12

Buried with him in baptism, in which you also were raised with Him through faith in the working of God, who raised Him from the dead.

Galatians 3:27

For as many of you as were baptized into Christ have put on Christ.

Romans 6:4-5

Therefore we were buried with Him through baptism into death, that just as Christ was raised from the dead by the glory of the Father, even so we also should walk in newness of life. For if we have been united together in the likeness of His death, certainly we also shall be in the likeness of His resurrection.

1 Corinthians 6:11
And such were some of you. But you were washed, but
you were sanctified, but you were justified in the name
of the Lord Jesus and by the Spirit of our God.

Jesus Saves Us (Acts 13:39, Gal.2:20 and 1Pet.3:18)

1 Timothy 1:15
This is a faithful saying, and worthy of all acceptance,
that Christ Jesus came into the world to save sinners, of
whom I am chief.

Hebrews 5:9
And having been perfected, He (Jesus) became the
author of eternal salvation to all who obey Him.

Acts 4:11-12
This is the 'stone which was rejected by you builders,
which has become the chief cornerstone.' Nor is there
salvation in any other, for there is no other name under
heaven given among men by which we must be saved."

God Saves Us

John 3:16
For God so loved the world that He gave His only
begotten Son, that whoever believes in Him should not
perish but have everlasting life.

Ephesians 2:4-5
But God, who is rich in mercy, because of His great love
with which He loved us, even when we were dead in

trespasses, made us alive together with Christ (by grace you have been saved).

1 Timothy 2:3-4
For this is good and acceptable in the sight of God our Savior, who desires all men to be saved and to come to the knowledge of the truth.

Hebrews 2:9
But we see Jesus, who was made a little lower than the angels, for the suffering of death crowned with glory and honor, that He, by the grace of God, might taste death for everyone.

Isaiah 12:2
Behold, God is my salvation,
I will trust and not be afraid;
For YAH, the Lord, is my strength and song;
He also has become my salvation.

1 Peter 1:3-4
Blessed be the God and Father of our Lord Jesus Christ, who according to His abundant mercy has begotten us again to a living hope through the resurrection of Jesus Christ from the dead to an inheritance incorruptible and undefiled and that does not fade away, reserved in heaven for you.

The Spirit Saves Us

1 Corinthians 6:11
And such were some of you. But you were washed, but you were sanctified, but you were justified in the name of the Lord Jesus and by the Spirit of our God.

Repentance Saves Us

Luke 13:3-5
I tell you, no; but unless you repent you will all likewise perish. Or those eighteen on whom the tower in Siloam fell and killed them, do you think that they were worse sinners than all other men who dwelt in Jerusalem? I tell you, no; but unless you repent you will all likewise perish."

Acts 2:38
Then Peter said to them, "Repent, and let every one of you be baptized in the name of Jesus Christ for the remission of sins; and you shall receive the gift of the Holy Spirit."

Acts 17:30
Truly, these times of ignorance God overlooked, but now commands all men everywhere to repent.

2 Corinthians 7:10
For godly sorrow produces repentance leading to salvation, not to be regretted; but the sorrow of the world produces death.

Acts 3:19

Repent therefore and be converted, that your sins may be blotted out, so that times of refreshing may come from the presence of the Lord.

Love Saves Us (The love God has for us and the love we have for God.)

John 3:16

For God so loved the world that He gave His only begotten Son, that whoever believes in Him should not perish but have everlasting life.

John 14:23

Jesus answered and said to him, "If anyone loves Me, he will keep My word; and My Father will love him, and We will come to him, and make Our home with him."

1 Corinthians 2:9

But as it is written:
"Eye has not seen, nor ear heard,
Nor have entered into the heart of man
The things which God has prepared for those who love Him."

Doing the Will of God Saves Us

1 John 2:17

And the world is passing away, and the lust of it; but he who does the will of God abides forever.

Walking in the Light Saves Us

1 John 1:7
But if we walk in the light as He is in the light, we have fellowship with one another, and the blood of Jesus Christ His Son cleanses us from all sin.

Mercy Saves Us

Titus 3:5
Not by works of righteousness which we have done, but according to His mercy He saved us, by the washing of regeneration and renewing of the Holy Spirit.

His Stripes/The Cross Saves Us (1 Peter 2:24-25)

Isaiah 53:5
But He was wounded for our transgressions,
He was bruised for our iniquities;
The chastisement for our peace was upon Him,
And by His stripes we are healed.

Galatians 6:14
But God forbid that I should boast except in the cross of our Lord Jesus Christ, by whom the world has been crucified to me, and I to the world.

Enduring Temptations Saves Us

James 1:12
Blessed is the man who endures temptation; for when he has been approved, he will receive the crown of life which the Lord has promised to those who love Him.

The Word Saves Us (John 5:24 and 1Cor. 15:1-2)

Romans 1:16

For I am not ashamed of the gospel of Christ, for it is the power of God to salvation for everyone who believes, for the Jew first and also for the Greek.

James 1:21

Therefore lay aside all filthiness and overflow of wickedness, and receive with meekness the implanted word, which is able to save your souls.

Acts 20:32

So now, brethren, I commend you to God and to the word of His grace, which is able to build you up and give you an inheritance among all those who are sanctified.

John 12:47-50

And if anyone hears My words and does not believe, I do not judge him; for I did not come to judge the world but to save the world. He who rejects Me, and does not receive My words, has that which judges him—the word that I have spoken will judge him in the last day. For I have not spoken on My own authority; but the Father who sent Me gave Me a command, what I should say and what I should speak. And I know that His command is everlasting life. Therefore, whatever I speak, just as the Father has told Me, so I speak.

Preaching Saves Us

1 Corinthians 1:21
For since, in the wisdom of God, the world through wisdom did not know God, it pleased God through the foolishness of the message preached to save those who believe.

Romans 10:13-15
For "whoever calls on the name of the Lord shall be saved." How then shall they call on Him in whom they have not believed? And how shall they believe in Him of whom they have not heard? And how shall they hear without a preacher? And how shall they preach unless they are sent? As it is written:
"How beautiful are the feet of those who preach the gospel of peace,
Who bring glad tidings of good things!"

Isaiah 52:7
How beautiful upon the mountains
Are the feet of him who brings good news,
Who proclaims peace,
Who brings glad tidings of good things,
Who proclaims salvation,
Who says to Zion, "Your God reigns!"

Matthew 28:19-20
Go therefore and make disciples of all the nations, baptizing them in the name of the Father and of the Son and of the Holy Spirit, teaching them to observe all things that I have commanded you; and lo, I am with you always, even to the end of the age." Amen.

Mark 16:15-16

And He said to them, "Go into all the world and preach the gospel to every creature. He who believes and is baptized will be saved; but he who does not believe will be condemned."

Matthew 9:37-38

Then He said to His disciples, "The harvest truly is plentiful, but the laborers are few. Therefore pray the Lord of the harvest to send out laborers into His harvest."

Confession Saves Us

Matthew 10:32-33

"Therefore whoever confesses Me before men, him I will also confess before My Father who is in heaven. But whoever denies Me before men, him I will also deny before My Father who is in heaven."

The Words that we Speak Save Us

Matthew 12:35-37

"A good man out of the good treasure of his heart brings forth good things, and an evil man out of the evil treasure brings forth evil things. But I say to you that for every idle word men may speak, they will give account of it in the day of judgment. For by your words you will be justified, and by your words you will be condemned."

Calling on the Name of the Lord Saves Us

Romans 10:13
For "whoever calls on the name of the Lord shall be saved."

I hope that you can see that there is much more to the gospel's plan for man's salvation than just isolating one verse and teaching it as a stand-alone doctrine! We are to honor "every word that proceeds from the mouth of God!"

Godly Sorrow Saves Us

2 Corinthians 7:9-10
Now I rejoice, not that you were made sorry, but that your sorrow led to repentance. For you were made sorry in a godly manner, that you might suffer loss from us in nothing. For godly sorrow produces repentance leading to salvation, not to be regretted; but the sorrow of the world produces death.

Obedience Saves Us (Romans 16:25-26 and John 15:14)

Hebrews 5:8-9
Though He was a Son, yet He learned obedience by the things which He suffered. And having been perfected, He became the author of eternal salvation to all who obey Him.

2 Thessalonians 1:7-8
...and to give you who are troubled rest with us when the Lord Jesus is revealed from heaven with His mighty angels, in flaming fire taking vengeance on those who do not know God, and on those who do not obey the gospel of our Lord Jesus Christ.

Endurance Saves Us (Hebrews 3:6)

Matthew 10:22
And you will be hated by all for My name's sake. But he who endures to the end will be saved.

Patience Saves Us

Hebrews 6:12
...that you do not become sluggish, but imitate those who through faith and patience inherit the promises.

Revelation 14:12-13
Here is the patience of the saints: here are those who keep the commandments of God and the faith of Jesus. Then I heard a voice from heaven saying to me, "Write: 'Blessed are the dead who die in the Lord from now on.'"

Belief Saves Us (John 5:24 and Acts 10:43)

John 3:36
"He who believes in the Son has everlasting life; and he who does not believe the Son shall not see life, but the wrath of God abides on him."

Love of the Truth Saves Us

2 Thessalonians 2:10
And with all unrighteous deception among those who perish, because they did not receive the love of the truth, that they might be saved.

Fear Saves (Acts 10:34-35)

Jude 1:22-23
And on some have compassion, making a distinction; but others save with fear, putting them out of the fire, hating even the garment defiled by the flesh.

Philippians 2:12
Therefore, my beloved, as you have always obeyed, not as in my presence only, but now much more in my absence, work out your own salvation with fear and trembling.

Save Ourselves

Acts 2:40
And with many other words he testified and exhorted them, saying, "Be saved from this perverse generation."

How do we save ourselves? The Bible tells us:

1 Timothy 4:16
Take heed to yourself and to the doctrine. Continue in them, for in doing this you will save both yourself and those who hear you.

Work Saves Us (John 5:29, Revelations 20:12-13 and Acts 10:34-35)

John 6:28-29

Then they said to Him, "What shall we do, that we may work the works of God?" Jesus answered and said to them, "This is the work of God, that you believe in Him whom He sent."

We will talk more about "works" in the next two sections.

Working Saves Us

Oh…. no…. I did not say that working saves us, did I? We have already established that God's word is very clear that a person cannot do anything that could **earn** him salvation. To illustrate this point let me tell you a story.

There are different versions of the following story, but I believe that all are equally powerful in driving home a tangible view on man earning or working for his salvation. The little story goes something like this…

One day you receive a phone call from Elon Musk. During the course of the conversation, he tells you that he would like to give you 44 billion dollars!!! Wow! Yahoo!

All that he asks for in return is that you come and pick him up at the airport and drive him to the bank so he can sign the check and get the funds transferred over to your account. Then he would like you to be an avid Tesla supporter, and tell others about how awesome a Tesla electric car is and how it can revolutionize their driving experience.

If you choose to commit yourself to this, Elon Musk is ready to give you 44 billion dollars.

Sounds great, right? Can you imagine the look on your face just after you see the bank statement that shows that you now have 44 billion dollars in your personal account?

Now, picture yourself announcing this wonderful event to your family and friends. You invite them all over for your big announcement. After dinner, you stand up, smiling from ear to ear you say, "I just EARNED/WORKED FOR AND WAS PAID 44 billion dollars from Elon Musk!"

Everyone, of course, thinks that you are joking, but after much convincing and displaying your new bank statement, they are finally all convinced. The most obvious next question everyone has is "How, how did you EARN 44 billion dollars?"

So, you tell them the whole story, starting at your rather unexpected phone call from Elon himself. You finish by telling them how hard you worked and how you earned and deserve the 44 billion dollars for all of your work!

Now this is just a story, but I hope that you can see how absolutely crazy and absurd it would be for you to make such a claim. You may have followed through on some conditions to your receiving such an inconceivable gift, but you in no way earned or deserved to be chosen or blessed with such a gift. And if your family and friends really loved and cared about you, hopefully someone would explain to you the reality of the situation.

Dear friend, the gift of your eternal life is so inconceivably greater than 44 billion dollars. It would be like comparing a speck of dust to the greatness of the known universe. For anyone to so degrade the gift of God in the life and death of His Son, by implying that you could ever do anything that would earn you the right to claim that you earned or deserved the gift of eternal life, is an absolute slap and spitting in the face of the Almighty Creator. And yet that is the exact objection you will hear as to why baptism does not save, because the religious world will claim, "It is a work!" So, in other words, if you let someone immerse you into water, now you worked for and earned your eternal salvation?!

A very natural correlation, right?! Let's not be absurd. People immerse themselves in water all the time and it is not considered a work. As a matter of fact, nine times out of ten, it is for fun and enjoyment.

We have already clearly seen that baptism/immersion is part of God's wonderful plan for man's salvation and is required to put us into Christ and forgive our sins. Let's also recall that Jesus Himself calls *belief* a work. And I hope that you can agree with me that belief and confession is far more difficult than letting someone dunk you in water.

John 6:28-29
Then they said to Him, "What shall we do, that we may work the works of God?" Jesus answered and said to them, "This is the work of God, that you believe in Him whom He sent."

Jesus also tells us that many will believe themselves saved because they feel that they did many good works in Jesus' name. But Jesus makes it clear that this is not enough, the works must be what were commanded by His Father. He then goes on to declare anything but

what the Father commands to be lawlessness! Read
Jesus' words for yourself. They are very clear and very
sobering, especially if you are not familiar with what
God commands you to do in His word.

> *Matthew 7:21-23*
> *"Not everyone who says to Me, 'Lord, Lord,' shall
> enter the kingdom of heaven, but he who does the will of
> My Father in heaven. Many will say to Me in that day,
> 'Lord, Lord, have we not prophesied in Your name,
> cast out demons in Your name, and done many wonders
> in Your name?' And then I will declare to them, 'I
> never knew you; depart from Me, you who practice
> lawlessness!'*

Here is a great quote to help us understand why it is so
difficult to help people embrace the truth once they
have already embraced a lie.

"Repeat a lie often enough and it becomes the truth," is
a law of propaganda, often attributed to the Nazi,
Joseph Goebbels.

I know this might be difficult for you to understand
because you have heard it often quoted.

> *Ephesians 2:8-9*
> *For by grace you have been saved through faith, and
> that not of yourselves; it is the gift of God, not of works,
> lest anyone should boast.*

First, does this say *GRACE ALONE*?

No, it says that we have been saved by *Grace*! Notice something else, Grace, through FAITH! Faith is our response to grace. If we believe/have faith in the death of Jesus Christ and the amazing gift offered to us because of Christ's shed blood, God offers us His Grace. He then sees Christ's shed perfect blood instead of our sins!

Secondly, what is being discussed here in Ephesians the second chapter?

What is the context? Please read Ephesians 2:10-22 and especially verse 15, underlined below.

Ephesians 2:10-22
For we are His workmanship, created in Christ Jesus for good works, which God prepared beforehand that we should walk in them. Therefore remember that you, once Gentiles in the flesh - who are called Uncircumcision by what is called the Circumcision made in the flesh by hands - that at that time you were without Christ, being aliens from the commonwealth of Israel and strangers from the covenants of promise, having no hope and without God in the world. But now in Christ Jesus you who once were far off have been brought near by the blood of Christ. For He Himself is our peace, who has made both one, and has broken down the middle wall of separation, <u>having abolished in His flesh the enmity, that is, the law of commandments contained in ordinances, so as to create in Himself one new man from the two, thus making peace,</u> and that He might reconcile them both to God in one body through the cross, thereby putting to death the enmity. And He came and preached

peace to you who were afar off and to those who were near. For through Him we both have access by one Spirit to the Father. Now, therefore, you are no longer strangers and foreigners, but fellow citizens with the saints and members of the household of God, having been built on the foundation of the apostles and prophets, Jesus Christ Himself being the chief cornerstone, in whom the whole building, being fitted together, grows into a holy temple in the Lord, in whom you also are being built together for a dwelling place of God in the Spirit.

Can you see that the context of these verses is in view of the works of the law? Is this not made clear by reading the whole passage? God is not declaring that man has no responsibility to obey His commands and work righteousness. He is showing that the works of the Law are no longer required. So, I ask you: Why are we trying to pit some scriptures against others, and teach this passage in such a way as to tell people that they have no actions or responsibilities before God? Because the book of James clearly says,

James 2:24
You see then that a man is justified by works, and not by faith only.

This passage is clear; we are to work. Just as Jesus clearly told those who came to Him and His Apostles.
Here are just two of many examples.

I ask you to not stop with these two passages, but to read the gospels and the book of Acts. You will be amazed to find that this is always Jesus and His apostles' response. And you will NEVER find either Jesus or His apostles saying, "What shall you do? Why, you can do nothing! You are saved by GRACE ALONE/ FAITH ONLY." They always instruct those who ask what they must do to be saved to DO something. Please don't take my word for it. Read it for yourself. This is not my belief. It is what is recorded in the Word of God.

Luke 10:25-37

And behold, a certain lawyer stood up and tested Him, saying, "Teacher, what shall I do to inherit eternal life?" He said to him, "What is written in the law? What is your reading of it?" So he answered and said, "'You shall love the Lord your God with all your heart, with all your soul, with all your strength, and with all your mind,' and 'your neighbor as yourself.'" And He said to him, "You have answered rightly; do this and you will live." But he, wanting to justify himself, said to Jesus, "And who is my neighbor?" Then Jesus answered and said: "A certain man went down from Jerusalem to Jericho, and fell among thieves, who stripped him of his clothing, wounded him, and departed, leaving him half dead. Now by chance a certain priest came down that road. And when he saw him, he passed by on the other side. Likewise a Levite, when he arrived at the place, came and looked, and passed by on the other side. But a certain Samaritan, as he journeyed, came where he was. And when he saw him, he had compassion. So he went to him and bandaged his wounds, pouring on oil and wine; and he set him on his own animal, brought him to an inn, and took care of him. On the next day, when he departed, he took out two denarii, gave them to

H. Roye

the innkeeper, and said to him, 'Take care of him; and whatever more you spend, when I come again, I will repay you.' So which of these three do you think was neighbor to him who fell among the thieves?" And he said, "He who showed mercy on him." Then Jesus said to him, "Go and do likewise."

In the above passage Jesus tells the man to love God and man. He then tells the parable of the Good Samaritan, in which the Samaritan does a good work. He concludes by saying, "Go and do likewise." Go and do something that shows that you love God and your fellow man! This surely sounds as if we are to do something. And in the example of the Samaritan, he personally went out of his way and did much on behalf of his fellow man!

Now, here is an example of the apostles being asked, "What shall we do?"

Notice that again the apostles respond in the affirmative. They must do something and proceeded to tell them what to do. Don't miss this! Read the passage and accept the words of God. After all, that is what belief is. So read and believe.

Acts 2:36-38
"Therefore let all the house of Israel know assuredly that God has made this Jesus, whom you crucified, both Lord and Christ." Now when they heard this, they were cut to the heart, and said to Peter and the rest of the apostles, "Men and brethren, what shall we do?" Then Peter said to them, "Repent, and let every one of you be

baptized in the name of Jesus Christ for the remission of sins; and you shall receive the gift of the Holy Spirit."

Friend, I want to ask you this question again, "What do Jesus and the apostles say when asked, 'What shall we do to inherit eternal life?'" The best way to answer this question would be for you to take the time to read the gospels and the book of Acts with this specific question in mind. I think that you will be surprised.

If you were asked the same question, "What shall we do to inherit eternal life?", what would your answer be? I bet you might say something like, "Do? Why you can do nothing! It is a free gift from God; we are saved by grace alone!"

Am I right? If I am, then I would like you to ask yourself, "Why is my answer different from the Lord's?" Do you think that it might be because you are not teaching the same gospel as Jesus and His apostles?

2 Peter 3:16
As also in all his epistles, speaking in them of these things, in which are some things hard to understand, which untaught and unstable people twist to their own destruction, as they do also the rest of the Scriptures.

Matthew 22:29
Jesus answered and said to them, "You are mistaken, not knowing the Scriptures nor the power of God.

1 Peter 4:11
If anyone speaks, let him speak as the oracles of God. If anyone ministers, let him do it as with the ability

which God supplies, that in all things God may be glorified through Jesus Christ, to whom belong the glory and the dominion forever and ever. Amen.

We must all ask ourselves these important questions: "Are you speaking as the oracles of God? Are you twisting the scriptures to fit man's doctrines? Are you mistaken because you have not studied enough to know all the scriptures and how they all work together?"

1 Peter 3:15
But sanctify the Lord God in your hearts, and always be ready to give a defense to everyone who asks you a reason for the hope that is in you, with meekness and fear.

2 Timothy 3:16-17
All Scripture is given by inspiration of God, and is profitable for doctrine, for reproof, for correction, for instruction in righteousness, that the man of God may be complete, thoroughly equipped for every good work.

Could the above passages be our answer as to why there is so much misunderstanding as to what God declares as His plan for man's salvation?

We should read again and listen well to J.C.Ryle.

"Man does not search the Scriptures! They do not dig into the wondrous mine of wisdom and knowledge and seek to become acquainted with its contents. Simple, regular reading of our Bible is the grand secret of establishment in the faith. Ignorance of the Scriptures is the root of all evil!"

James 2:24
You see then that a man is justified by works, and not by faith only.

This is such an important point that we will restate it again. Here it is, the only time that FAITH ONLY is used in the whole Bible. Do not miss the tiny little word that is found right before it: NOT. So here we have the only time *faith only* is used and it says the opposite of what is proclaimed as God's plan for man's salvation. We see it clearly stated that we are NOT SAVED BY FAITH ONLY!

We'll Work 'til Jesus Comes: We Will Work!

Acts 10:34-35
Then Peter opened his mouth and said: "In truth I
perceive that God shows no partiality. But in every
nation whoever fears Him and works righteousness is
accepted by Him.

We are to *work* righteousness! I saved, "Works Save Us"
for last because I believe it will be the most difficult.
Why? Because you have heard thousands of times, "You
can do nothing, faith only, grace only, grace alone, it's
not about what you have done but what Christ has
already done, etc...."

These statements give you the deceptive understanding
that no matter what you do, you will still be saved. Please
Friend, is this what the word of God teaches? When
Jesus Himself was asked in the gospels, "What must I
do to inherit eternal life/be saved?" What was our
Lord's answer? Did He say, "You can do nothing, your
salvation is not of works, you are saved by grace alone,
it is not about what you choose or do, but about My
work on the cross"? You will not read these words in
the gospel accounts. Jesus answered this question many
times throughout the gospels, and He always answered
with the affirmative that they must do something and
states specifically what they must do.

Philippians 2:12
Therefore, my beloved, as you have always obeyed, not
as in my presence only, but now much more in my

absence, work out your own salvation with fear and trembling.

Now Friend, the Bible commands you here to "work out". No, not at the gym. We must work out our own salvation. And we are commanded to work it out in fear and trembling.

Romans 2:5-10

But in accordance with your hardness and your impenitent heart you are treasuring up for yourself wrath in the day of wrath and revelation of the righteous judgment of God, who "will render to each one according to his deeds": eternal life to those who by patient continuance in doing good seek for glory, honor, and immortality; but to those who are self-seeking and do not obey the truth, but obey unrighteousness - indignation and wrath, tribulation and anguish, on every soul of man who does evil, of the Jew first and also of the Greek; but glory, honor, and peace to everyone who works what is good, to the Jew first and also to the Greek.

Revelation 20:12

And I saw the dead, small and great, standing before God, and books were opened. And another book was opened, which is the Book of Life. And the dead were judged according to their works, by the things which were written in the books.

Matthew 12:36-37

But I say to you that for every idle word men may speak, they will give account of it in the day of judgment. For

*by your words you will be justified, and by your words
you will be condemned.*

Make no mistake, we will be judged, *according to our works.*
Even what we choose to say shall justify us or condemn
us. These are Jesus Christ's words not man's.
As we read through these verses, let's be careful to note
that God has not decided ahead of time who is saved
and who is lost. God has clearly shown us that man
decides his eternal destiny. When God addresses the
elect/chosen/those predestined to salvation/sealed in
Christ, He has already defined what He means by these
titles and we are not at liberty to redefine them for Him.

John 6:27
*Do not labor for the food which perishes, but for the
food which endures to everlasting life, which the Son of
Man will give you, because God the Father has set His
seal on Him.*

John 6:27 is our answer to the question; Who did God
elect/predestine/choose/seal? The passage tells us that
it is "those who labor for the food that endures to
everlasting life!" Jesus Christ clearly teaches that it is our
choices and actions which determine our eternity. Our
destiny is determined every day by the choices that we
make to follow God or follow man.

Acts 10:34-35
*Then Peter opened his mouth and said: "In truth I
perceive that God shows no partiality. But in every
nation whoever fears Him and works righteousness is
accepted by Him.*

God defines what it means to be His elect/predestined/chosen/sealed in Christ. Those that **fear God and work righteousness.** If you inquire of others what the definition of the elect is, you will find that they may give you a very different definition. So the ultimate question is who will you believe: God or man? Choose wisely, because your salvation depends on it!

> *Luke 13:24*
> *Strive to enter through the narrow gate, for many, I say to you, will seek to enter and will not be able.*

Strive means *to make great efforts to achieve or obtain something, to struggle or fight vigorously.* Sounds like work, wouldn't you agree? Jesus commands us that we are to do just that if we seek to enter into heaven!

> *John 5:28-29*
> *Do not marvel at this; for the hour is coming in which all who are in the graves will hear His voice and come forth—those who have done good, to the resurrection of life, and those who have done evil, to the resurrection of condemnation.*

Here in John, we see again that our choices determine our future destination, either into the presence of God or eternal separation from Him!

> *Matthew 16:27*
> *For the Son of Man will come in the glory of His Father with His angels, and then He will reward each according to his works.*

Ask yourself, "If my works truly do not matter, then why is the Lord declaring that you will be rewarded according to your works?"

Hebrews 4:11
Let us therefore be diligent to enter that rest, lest anyone fall according to the same example of disobedience.

Hebrews tells us that if we do not labor, we are showing our unbelief. In other words, true belief is always accompanied by our actions. Do your actions proclaim your obedience to our Almighty God? Or do they proclaim the doctrines of men?

God is not trying to confuse us or give us the wrong impression, neither does His word contradict itself. We are going to be judged by our works and rewarded according to our works. We are also commanded to labor to enter His rest. And as we all know to labor is to work.

H. Roye

PART 3

From Genesis to Revelation

Has God always had conditions on whether we are accepted or not? The answer is YES, from Genesis to Revelation, God is the same. When man chooses to obey, then he is accepted by God!

Let's look at some examples. Adam and Eve were put in Eden, or Paradise, and were given terms or conditions by which they would be able to remain in Paradise. If they did not obey the conditions, they would lose Paradise. Well, we know the way that one turned out. Let's think about this for a minute. Did Adam and Eve earn the right to remain in Paradise by their obedience? The Bible makes it clear that this is not the case. They did not deserve to live in Paradise or earn it based on their actions. However, if they wished to remain in Paradise, they had to fulfill the conditions put on them by God. God from the very beginning set forth His plan for man and makes it clear that the responsibility is man's to either remain *in Him* or to rebel by disobedience and choose not to remain *in Him*. Cain is another excellent example.

Genesis 4:5-7
But He did not respect Cain and his offering. And Cain was very angry, and his countenance fell. So the Lord said to Cain, "Why are you angry? And why has your countenance fallen? If you do well, will you not be accepted? And if you do not do well, sin lies at the door. And its desire is for you, but you should rule over it."

128

Was Abel God's elect or chosen and not Cain? God made it clear that this was not the case, but that Cain had a choice. It was his responsibility and what he chose determined his future. God tells Cain, rather pleads with him to *do well* and then he would be accepted, too. God further pleads with Cain to rule over the sin he is tempted by. He wants Cain to be blessed and succeed, but ultimately it is Cain's choice. Cain chose to sin and reaped the consequence of his choice in verse 14, being driven out from the face of the earth and the face of God. God has declared to us that He does not change; He is the same yesterday, today and forever.

Hebrews 13:8
Jesus Christ is the same yesterday, today, and forever.

Our God is consistent in the way that He chooses to interact with us; He has not changed.
Now, let's jump ahead a few chapters in Genesis and look at the message we find in the story of Noah.

Genesis 6:5-13
Then the Lord saw that the wickedness of man was great in the earth, and that every intent of the thoughts of his heart was only evil continually. And the Lord was sorry that He had made man on the earth, and He was grieved in His heart. So the Lord said, "I will destroy man whom I have created from the face of the earth, both man and beast, creeping thing and birds of the air, for I am sorry that I have made them." But Noah found grace in the eyes of the Lord. This is the genealogy of Noah. Noah was a just man, perfect in his

> *generations. Noah walked with God. And Noah begot
> three sons: Shem, Ham, and Japheth. The earth also
> was corrupt before God, and the earth was filled with
> violence. So God looked upon the earth, and indeed it
> was corrupt; for all flesh had corrupted their way on the
> earth. And God said to Noah, "The end of all flesh
> has come before Me, for the earth is filled with violence
> through them; and behold, I will destroy them with the
> earth.*

This passage is hard to understand if you are trying to fit it into the teachings and doctrines of God electing or choosing you apart from your own choice or actions, or that your works have no bearing on your salvation. Let's simply read the passage and ask ourselves was Noah the only one that God chose to elect during this time in history? We also should wonder at the fact that God is "sorry and grieved in His heart that He created man." If God is the one who elects the chosen based on His good pleasure, not upon whether man obeys or chooses not to obey, then what happened here? Did our all-powerful God just forget to elect anyone and then get upset with man because He couldn't remember to elect anyone during this time in history? OR was Noah chosen based upon his action and obedience to God? I think if we are honest, we will simply take this passage at face value and acknowledge that Noah was saved because of his obedience. Now don't get crazy here and throw the baby out with the bath water. Nowhere do we see Noah saying that he earned his salvation (keep in mind that it took him about 100 years to build the ark and that during this time, the Bible calls him a preacher of righteousness). Sounds like Noah worked pretty hard to me, yet he realized that it was God who saved him and he in no way earned/deserved the salvation granted to him. He worshipped God and gave Him the credit for His salvation (Genesis 8:20). The Bible is literally full of examples of man's salvation being based upon man choosing God by *fearing God and working righteousness* (Acts10:34-35). Notice the choice of words here: we are to work!

> ### John 6:27-29
> *"Do not labor for the food which perishes, but for the food which endures to everlasting life, which the Son of Man will give you, because God the Father has set His seal on Him." Then they said to Him, "What shall we do, that we may work the works of God?" Jesus answered and said to them, "This is the work of God, that you believe in Him whom He sent."*

I want to take a minute to remind you that Jesus Himself, when asked, calls even belief a work that man must do to work the works of God. Hebrews also mentions…

> ### Hebrews 11:6
> *But without faith it is impossible to please Him, for he who comes to God must believe that He is, and that He is a rewarder of those who diligently seek Him.*

Who does God say that He rewards? Those who *diligently seek Him.* Sounds like work, would you not agree?

1 John 1:6-8

If we say that we have fellowship with Him, and walk in darkness, we lie and do not practice the truth. But if we walk in the light as He is in the light, we have fellowship with one another, and the blood of Jesus Christ His Son cleanses us from all sin. If we say that we have no sin, we deceive ourselves, and the truth is not in us.

Friend, please consider that this passage is addressed to Christians, and we are told that we are covered by the blood of Christ if we choose to *walk in the light.* If that were not clear enough, God also mentioned that if we say that we have fellowship with God and yet continue to walk in darkness, we are a liar and do not know the truth!

1 John 1:9

If we confess our sins, He is faithful and just to forgive us our sins and to cleanse us from all unrighteousness.

God has further clarified that we must do something! We must confess our sins and then *He is faithful and just to forgive us our sins.* I really hope that the importance of our actions and choices in our salvation and our daily Christian walk is becoming unavoidably clear as we read through God's word.

Now let's walk through two chapters in the word of God before we conclude on the topic of works, our choices, or our actions saving us or condemning us. The following passages clarify that works do not save. Why, because the works referred to are the works of the old

Law, which are done apart from the blood of Jesus Christ. We already studied that it is the blood of Jesus Christ that saves and justifies. So works of the Old Law without Christ's cleansing blood will never save and were never intended to replace the blood of Christ.

Galatians 3:1

O foolish Galatians! Who has bewitched you that you should not obey the truth, before whose eyes Jesus Christ was clearly portrayed among you as crucified?

Paul says that we can be deceived, causing us to not obey the truth. The sobering thing is that they saw the events take place and they still chose not to obey the truth. Next, please notice what the word of God is addressing when it is talking about works. This passage is a beautiful example God has given us because He does not desire for us to be confused. The works that do not save are the works of the Old Law.

Galatians 3:2-3

This only I want to learn of you: Did you receive the Spirit by the works of the law, or by the hearing of faith? Are you so foolish? Having begun in the Spirit, are you now being made perfect by the flesh?

Christians were forgetting that Christ's death was the completion of the Old Law and the works that were commanded in it. We see in the next verse that if you try to justify yourself by the Old Law, your faith is made vain. Our faith is no longer to be in the things written in the Old Law but in Jesus Christ. Also consider that a

Christian can make their suffering for Christ vain/useless.

Galatians 3:4-10

Have you suffered so many things in vain – if indeed it was in vain? Therefore He who supplies the Spirit to you and works miracles among you, does He do it by the works of the law, or by the hearing of faith? – just as Abraham "believed God, and it was accounted to him for righteousness." Therefore know that only those who are of faith are sons of Abraham. And the Scripture, foreseeing that God would justify the Gentiles by faith, preached the gospel to Abraham beforehand, saying, "In you all nations shall be blessed." So then those who are of faith are blessed with believing Abraham. For as many as are of the works of the law are under the curse; for it is written, "Cursed is everyone who does not continue in all things which are written in the book of the law, to do them."

If we wanted to be justified by the Old Law, we would have to fulfill all the law perfectly. But even that does not justify us in the sight of God.

Galatians 3:11-21
But that no one is justified by the law in the sight of God is evident, for "the just shall live by faith." Yet the law is not of faith, but "the man who does them shall live by them." Christ has redeemed us from the curse of the law, having become a curse for us (for it is written, "cursed is everyone who hangs on a tree"), that the blessing of Abraham might come upon the Gentiles in

Christ Jesus, that we might receive the promise of the Spirit through faith. Brethren, I speak in the manner of men: Though it is only a man's covenant, yet if it is confirmed, no one annuls or adds to it. Now to Abraham and his Seed were the promises made. He does not say, "And to seeds," as of many, but as of one, "And to your Seed," who is Christ. And this I say, that the law, which was four hundred and thirty years later, cannot annul the covenant that was confirmed before by God in Christ, that it should make the promise of no effect. For if the inheritance is of the law, it is no longer of promise; but God gave it to Abraham by promise. What purpose then does the law serve? It was added because of transgressions, till the Seed should come to whom the promise was made; and it was appointed through angels by the hand of a mediator. Now a mediator does not mediate for one only, but God is one. Is the law then against the promises of God? Certainly not! For if there had been a law given which could have given life, truly righteousness would have been by the law.

The Old Law and the works required could not give life, that is why righteousness cannot be gained by the works of the law.

Galatians 3:22-25

But the Scripture has confined all under sin, that the promise by faith in Jesus Christ might be given to those who believe. But before faith came, we were kept under guard by the law, kept for the faith which would afterward be revealed. Therefore the law was our tutor

to bring us to Christ, that we might be justified by faith.
But after faith has come, we are no longer under a tutor.

This is why we do not keep the Old Law and the works required by it. The Old Law was simply our tutor (KJV says "school master"), leading us to Jesus Christ. So when we get to Galatians 3:26-27 we can clearly see the difference between the works of the law and the works of faith which put us into Christ.

Galatians 3: 26-27
For you are all sons of God through faith in Christ Jesus.
For as many of you as were baptized into Christ have put on Christ.

Please, don't miss how we are put into Christ! The question is, "Do you wish to be put into Christ?"

Remember, all of God's promises of salvation and blessings are given to those that are IN CHRIST! If you have not been baptized, you are NOT in Christ! And if you have been baptized, but for the wrong reason because you did not understand this truth, then be baptized again! That is the example left to us in God's word!

Acts 19:1-5
And it happened, while Apollos was at Corinth, that Paul, having passed through the upper regions, came to Ephesus. And finding some disciples he said to them, "Did you receive the Holy Spirit when you believed?" So they said to him, "We have not so much as heard

*whether there is a Holy Spirit." And he said to them,
"Into what then were you baptized?" So they said,
"Into John's baptism." Then Paul said, "John indeed
baptized with a baptism of repentance, saying to the
people that they should believe on Him who would come
after him, that is, on Christ Jesus," When they heard
this, they were baptized in the name of the Lord Jesus.*

Let us pick up again in…

Galatians 3:28-29
*There is neither Jew nor Greek, there is neither slave
nor free, there is neither male nor female: for you are all
one in Christ Jesus. And if you are Christ's, then you
are Abraham's seed, and heirs according to the promise.*

Again, if it was not made clear enough, God restates that
we are only heirs according to the promise if we are
Christ's. I have included later a list of verses that state
the importance of being *IN CHRIST*.

I want to remind you that we are looking at these
passages to see that we are not to perform the works of
the law. The references to works in the Bible are talking
about the works of the Old Law, not the conditions for
salvation found under Christ and the New Testament.
Both Galatians 3 and Hebrews 10 show these concepts
side by side.

Hebrews 10:1-9
*For the law having a shadow of the good things to come,
and not the very image of the things, can never*

with these same sacrifices, which they offer continually year by year, make those who approach perfect. For then would they not have ceased to be offered? For the worshippers, once purified, would have had no more consciousness of sins. But in those sacrifices there is a reminder of sins every year. For it is not possible that the blood of bulls and goats could take away sins. Therefore, when He came into the world, He said: "Sacrifice and offering you did not desire, but a body you have prepared for me. In burnt offerings and sacrifices for sin you had no pleasure. Then I said, 'Behold, I have come – in the volume of the book it is written of me – to do Your will, O God.'" Previously saying, "Sacrifice and offering, burnt offerings, and offerings for sin You did not desire, nor had pleasure in them" (which are offered according to the law), then He said, "Behold, I have come to do Your will, O God." He takes away the first that He may establish the second.

I believe that you will find the above Scriptures basic and easy to follow. It simply states that the Old Law was never intended to permanently remove sins. Christ was always the permanent plan for man's salvation. God always planned on taking away the works and requirements of the Old Law. Jesus Himself taught this concept to the women at the well.

John 4:20-26
Our fathers worshiped on this mountain, and you Jews say that in Jerusalem is the place where one ought to worship." Jesus said to her, "Woman, believe Me, the hour is coming when you will neither on this mountain,

nor in Jerusalem, worship the Father. You worship what you do not know; we know what we worship, for salvation is of the Jews. But the hour is coming, and now is, when the true worshipers will worship the Father in spirit and truth; for the Father is seeking such to worship Him. God is Spirit, and those who worship Him must worship in spirit and truth." The woman said to Him, "I know that Messiah is coming" (who is called Christ). "When He comes, He will tell us all things." Jesus said to her, "I who speak to you am He."

God has always desired the hearts of men to worship Him in Spirit and truth.

Hebrews 10: 10-14
By that will we have been sanctified through the offering of the body of Jesus Christ once and for all. And every priest stands ministering daily and offering repeatedly the same sacrifices, which can never take away sins. But this Man, after he had offered one sacrifice for sins forever, sat down at the right hand of God, from that time waiting till His enemies are made His footstool. For by one offering He has perfected forever those who are being sanctified.

Here we have the same question, how are we sanctified and perfected? Again, we are sanctified and perfected by Jesus Christ, offering Himself up on the cross.

Hebrews 10:15-39
But the Holy Spirit also witnesses to us; for after He had said before, "This is the covenant that I will make with them after those days, says the LORD: I will put

My laws into their hearts, and in their minds I will write them", then He adds, "Their sins and their lawless deeds I will remember no more." Now where there is remission of these, there is no longer an offering for sin. Therefore, brethren, having boldness to enter the Holiest by the blood of Jesus, by a new and living way which he consecrated for us, through the veil, that is, His flesh, and having a High Priest over the house of God, let us draw near with a true heart in full assurance of faith, <u>having our hearts sprinkled from an evil conscience and our bodies washed with pure water.</u> Let us hold fast the confession of our hope without wavering, for He who promised is faithful. And let us consider one another in order to stir up love and good works, not forsaking the assembling of ourselves together, as is the manner of some, but exhorting one another, and so much the more as you see, the Day approaching. <u>For if we sin willfully after we have received the knowledge of the truth, there no longer remains a sacrifice for sins, but a certain fearful expectation of judgment, and fiery indignation, which will devour the adversaries.</u> Anyone who has rejected Moses' law dies without mercy on the testimony of two or three witnesses. <u>Of how much worse punishment do you suppose, will he be thought worthy who has trampled the Son of God underfoot, counted the blood of the covenant by which he was sanctified a common thing, and insulted the Spirit of grace?</u> For we know Him who said, "Vengeance is Mine, I will repay," says the Lord. And again, the Lord will judge his people." It is a fearful thing to fall into the hands of the living God. <u>But recall the former days in which, after you were illuminated, you endured a great struggle with sufferings: partly while you were made a spectacle</u> both *by reproaches and tribulations, and partly while you became companions of those who were so treated; for you had compassion on me in my chains, and joyfully accepted the plundering of your goods, knowing that you have a better and an enduring possession for yourselves in heaven. <u>Therefore do not cast away your confidence, which has great reward. For you have need of endurance, so that after you have done the will of God, you may receive the promise:</u> "For yet a little while, and He who is coming will come and will not tarry. <u>Now the just shall live by faith; but if anyone draws back, my soul has no pleasure in him." But we are not of those who draw back to perdition, but of those who believe to the saving of the soul.</u>*

As we wrap up the topic of works, I hope that God's Word has made several things clear.

#1- We are not saved by the works of the law.

#2- Nothing that we do will save us apart from the blood of Jesus Christ.

#3- We must fulfill the conditions set upon us by God to be put into Christ so that His blood will cleanse us. 1 John 1:6-8

#4- To remain in Christ, we must obey what He has asked and continue to choose to walk in righteousness. 1 John 1:6-10

It is very important that we focus on the words and instructions of God and that we do not get hung up on men's doctrines. The word of God tells us over and over again that good works are expected of the Christian, and indeed, if one does not have good works, it shows that he is not a follower of Jesus Christ.

I hope that this brief overview of a few passages has whet your appetite to discover and read for yourself the hundreds of examples that are contained within God's word. Here are a few more Scriptures for you to look up. All I ask is that you simply ask yourself, "Does man have work and responsibility to receive salvation?" What do you see in the following verses?

Genesis 7:1; 18:19 & 25
Deuteronomy 28:58
Joshua 24:15
1 Samuel 13:13; 15:19, 22-23
2 Kings 14:6
1 Chronicles 29:17-18
Psalms 28:4-5; 28:13; 101; 119:173
Proverbs 2; 21:21; 28:5-9
Isaiah 1:15-20; 5:3-6
Jeremiah 4:1; 3:12-13; 7:23-28; 17:1-10
Ezekiel 9
Hosea 4:6
Matthew 5:28-29
Luke 15:32
John 14:15 & 23
Romans 6:16
Galatians 6:7-10
Ephesians 1:13
Colossians 1:23
Hebrews 12:17

1 Peter 1:17
1 John 3:12
Revelation 20:12-13

After reading these verses, you will be able to proclaim that the Bible addresses the sinner in a way that makes his eternal damnation or salvation his responsibility and choice. God has not forced salvation on anyone. Everyone who is lost, is lost because of their own choice. (Hebrews 10:36-39) There is no *"once saved always saved"*. You may walk away from God or choose to walk towards Him. Your attitude and humble heart of obedience is all that is asked. You will fall, make mistakes, and have really bad days, but the good news is that Christ's blood is perfect enough to cleanse you and cover any sin as long as your attitude is one that is seeking Him. Remember Jonah; we cannot hide from God or deceive Him. He sees your heart of obedience or rebellion! (Ezekiel 18:21-24)

Psalm 119:105
Your word is a lamp to my feet, and a light to my path.

I truly hope that your eyes are being opened and your heart is learning to be tuned by God's word. We have seen repeatedly that God's word proclaims us to be saved by many things, faith and grace being only a part of that perfect harmony. For anyone to isolate faith and grace and teach it as the gospel plan of salvation to the exclusion of all the other elements taught in the word of God, is rebellion to God and His Word. Let us learn every day to *live by every word that proceeds from the mouth of God* (Matthew 4:4).

Remember, if God has told us in His word that faith saves us, yet later tells us that baptism saves us, these are not two separate teachings. They are just two different elements needed for the salvation of mankind. Baptism is implied in the faith verse and faith is implied in the baptism verse. If we choose to pick and choose the Scriptures that we want and throw out or ignore the ones we don't, we are not honoring God or His Word. All Scripture is written of God and equally as important. (Please take the time to reread the quotes from J.C. Ryle on the back cover of this book)

> *2 Timothy 3:16*
> *All Scripture is given by inspiration of God, and is profitable for doctrine, for reproof, for correction, for instruction in righteousness.*

It is our responsibility to study to understand how all of God's Word fits together perfectly to reprove, correct and instruct us in righteousness. Let's never be found trying to make God's commands and truths contradict each other.

> *Isaiah 12:2*
> *Behold, God is my salvation;*
> *I will trust, and not be afraid:*
> *For YAH, the LORD JEHOVAH is my strength and my song;*
> *He also has become my salvation'.*

1 Peter 1:3-4
Blessed be the God and Father of our Lord Jesus Christ, who according to His abundant mercy has begotten us again to a living hope through the resurrection of Jesus Christ from the dead, to an inheritance incorruptible and undefiled and that does not fade away, reserved in heaven for you.

It is wonderful to see the variety of things working together (pages 95-110) that God says work out our salvation, and the ease and simplicity of what He has asked us to do. If someone were to ask me as they did on the day of Pentecost, "What must I do to be saved?" I believe that God's word has shown by the above commands, statements and personal examples that the only way to be brought into contact with the blood of Christ, and thus to be put into Christ, is to follow these commands.

Acts 2:38
Then Peter said to them, "Repent, and let every one of you be baptized in the name of Jesus Christ for the remission of sins; and you shall receive the gift of the Holy Spirit."

Acts 22:16
And now why are you waiting? Arise and be baptized, and wash away your sins, calling on the name of the Lord.

Finding the Treasure

Starting with Noah, there was one door (Christ) and all that entered in were saved. Noah believed and obeyed for a hundred years while he was building the ark and yet you never see him saying, "I earned my salvation." He understood that though he obeyed and worked, that could never have given him the right before a Holy God to earn anything. We then see the picture of baptism as they were saved through water and the water cleansed the earth of sin.

God gives us the same picture of our salvation, that in baptism the sin is cleansed or washed away.

Acts 22:16
And now why are you waiting? Arise and be baptized, and wash away your sins, calling on the name of the Lord.

1 Peter 3:20-21
...who formerly were disobedient, when once the Divine longsuffering waited in the days of Noah, while the ark was being prepared, in which a few, that is, eight souls, were saved through water. There is also an antitype which now saves us — baptism (not the removal of the filth of the flesh, but the answer of a good conscience toward God).

Then there is the wonderful example of the children of Israel as they were in Egypt. The blood saved them so that they were passed over by the angel of death. They were then set free from their bondage when they passed through the Red Sea and were baptized in the waters, the Lord then caused the waters to destroy the bondage (sin) that followed them (the Egyptians).

> *1 Corinthians 10:1-4*
> *Moreover, brethren, I do not want you to be unaware that all our fathers were under the cloud, all passed through the sea, all were baptized into Moses in the cloud and in the sea, all ate the same spiritual food, and all drank the same spiritual drink. For they drank of that spiritual Rock that followed them, and that Rock was Christ.*

I love all these examples because they show us such a clear picture of God's plan from Genesis to Revelation. The foreshadowing in the Old Testament is truly amazing. I enjoyed revisiting these great passages and the beautiful message of life and hope that they contain!

But…What About…?

All right, so as promised, let's look at your objections to water baptism being required to put man into Jesus Christ. I am guessing that the following will be an answer to some of your mental objections to water baptism. Let's dig in and take a look at what God's Word teaches. We will start by addressing the thief on the cross because it is brought up consistently as a reason why baptism does not save you.

First, the thief died under the old covenant (It would not be possible to be buried with Christ according to Romans 6, when Christ had not died).

Hebrews 9:15-17
And for this reason He is the Mediator of the new covenant, by means of death, for the redemption of the transgressions under the first covenant, that those who are called may receive the promise of the eternal inheritance. For where there is a testament, there must also of necessity be the death of the testator. <u>For a testament is in force after men are dead, since it has no power at all while the testator lives.</u>

So as the scripture states, we were not under the covenant of faith until after Christ died. Before He died, the Old Law was still the vessel of salvation. Again, we cannot reenact the death of Jesus Christ until after He has died and shed His blood.

Second, Jesus had the power on earth to forgive sins.

Luke 7:48-50
Then He said to her, "Your sins are forgiven." And those who sat at the table with Him began to say to themselves, "Who is this who even forgives sins?" Then He said to the woman, "Your faith has saved you. Go in peace."

Luke 5:20-24
When He saw their faith, He said to him, "Man, your sins are forgiven you." And the scribes and the Pharisees began to reason, saying, "Who is this who speaks blasphemies? Who can forgive sins but God alone?" But when Jesus perceived their thoughts, He answered and said to them, "Why are you reasoning in your hearts? Which is easier, to say, 'Your sins are forgiven you,' or to say, 'Rise up and walk'? But that you may know that the Son of Man has power on earth to forgive sins" - He said to the man who was paralyzed, "I say to you, arise, take up your bed, and go to your house."

We must remember that Jesus Christ is God and as He stated, *"the Son of Man has power on earth to forgive sins."*

And last, but not least, it is curious to me that it is assumed that the thief was not baptized by John the Baptist. Let's just read the passage and evaluate the information that we are given.

Luke 23:39-43
And one of the criminals who were hanged blasphemed Him, saying, "If You are the Christ, save Yourself and us." But the other, answering, rebuked him saying, "Do

> *you not even fear God, seeing you are under the same condemnation? And we indeed justly, for we received the due reward of our deeds; <u>but this Man has done nothing wrong.</u>" Then he said to Jesus, "<u>Lord, remember me when you come into Your Kingdom.</u>" And Jesus said to him, "Assuredly, I say to you, today you will be with Me in Paradise."*

Historically, Romans did not crucify Romans, so the man could very well have been a Jew. The passage reveals to us that he fears God and understands just punishment for crimes. Next, we see he is confident that Jesus has done nothing wrong or worthy of death, making it obvious that he knew Jesus and His character. He also understood that Jesus was here to establish His kingdom. I believe that after carefully looking at all this information, it would be safe to say that the man had a good chance of being a Jew, and furthermore heard Jesus' teachings and John the Baptist's. That being said, why are we assuming that he was not baptized as commanded by John the Baptist and Jesus and His disciples? It is highly probable given the facts that we are given, the man did believe, was baptized and then fell from his convictions and committed some crime.

The following passages state that the baptisms of John the Baptist and Jesus were *of repentance for the remission of sins* and we can see that Jesus, His disciples, and John the Baptist were all immersing/baptizing.

> *Luke 3:3*
> *And he went into all the region around Jordan, preaching a baptism of repentance for the remission of sins.*
>
> *John 3:22-26*
> *After these things Jesus and his disciples came into the land of Judaea, and there he remained with them and baptized. Now John also was baptizing in Aenon near Salim, because there was much water there. And they came and were baptized. For John had not yet been thrown into prison. Then there arose a dispute between some of John's disciples and the Jews about purification. And they came to John, and said to him, "Rabbi, He who was with you beyond the Jordan, to whom you have testified - behold, He is baptizing, and all are coming to Him!"*

I hope that after reading the passages regarding the thief on the cross you see that it is more probable that the thief was baptized and knew Jesus, then the common thought that he was not baptized and knew nothing of Jesus until the crucifixion. The point is that we don't know for sure and that assumptions can cause us to ignore the facts that are clearly given. It is my hope that after reading the above three points, you can safely say that the thief on the cross is not a logical or Biblical example of someone being saved apart from baptism!

Remember the first point, THE THIEF ON THE CROSS DIED UNDER THE OLD LAW.

Next, let's look at a scenario that I have heard from those wishing to reject the role that immersion/ baptism plays in our salvation. The objection goes something like this: what if you were in the car on the way to be baptized and you were killed in a car accident? What then? Does the person die in their sins, since they were not put into Christ and their sins were not washed away?

First of all, it is important that we never try and disprove the word of God by life experiences, that is why we are called to a life of faith, trust and obedience. And secondly, that same question can be asked this way: what if you are a missionary and you come upon someone dying in a field? You rush to them and ask if they have heard about Jesus, and they have not. You then start to tell them the wonderful news about the Savior who came to die for their sins, but before you are able to tell them everything so that they might believe, they die! What then? The answer to the second scenario is the same as the answer to the first! The answer is that we have a merciful and gracious God and that He sees a heart turning towards Him in understanding, repentance, and obedience. The scriptural answer to the situation is found in Luke 15:11-32. We see here that the father runs to the prodigal son while he is still a long way off! God's desire has always been a humble heart that is seeking to obey Him, and God sees the heart. He will not be fooled; He is well aware that both of the above individuals are seeking Him and this is what He desires.

2 Chronicles 7:14
If my people who are called by My name will humble themselves, and pray and seek My face, and turn from

their wicked ways, then I will hear from heaven, and will forgive their sin and heal their land.

2 Chronicles 16:9
For the eyes of the Lord run to and fro throughout the whole earth, to show Himself strong on behalf of those whose heart is loyal toward Him. In this you have done foolishly; therefore from now on you shall have wars.

The Bible declares to us that He will not cast out those who are earnestly seeking Him, even if they do not currently have all the truth. However, this is no excuse to purposefully be disobedient to the commands of God because of our own choosing.

Romans 6:1
What shall we say then? Shall we continue in sin that grace may abound?

Romans 6: 16-18
Do you not know that to whom you present yourselves slaves to obey, you are that one's slaves whom you obey, whether of sin leading to death, or of obedience leading to righteousness? But God be thanked that though you were slaves of sin, yet you obeyed from the heart that form of doctrine to which you were delivered. And having been set free from sin, you became slaves of righteousness.

Since we are dealing with objections to immersion/ baptism, we should also address the conversion of Cornelius. Because it is claimed that since the Holy Spirit came on him prior to baptism, he must have been saved prior to baptism, since the sign of the Holy Spirit was the promised gift.

Acts 2:38
Then Peter said unto them, "Repent, and let every one of you be baptized in the name of Jesus Christ for the remission of sins, and you shall receive the gift of the Holy Spirit."

First, let's note that the above verse is the Biblical pattern throughout the New Testament. People believed, repented, confessed and were immersed/ baptized after which they received the gift of the Holy Spirit. The only exception is when Cornelius and the Gentiles were going to be accepted into the church. The Holy Spirit came upon them as a sign to show those of the circumcision that God now accepts the Gentiles. This is not my translation of the verse: it is what is said if we read the account. Also, it is important to notice that Peter was to speak to them *words by which they might be saved*, and that the Holy Spirit fell upon them, *as he began to speak.* So, the Holy Spirit was poured out before they even had a chance to believe anything about Jesus Christ. In this one case the Holy Spirit came upon Cornelius and his family prior to belief, repentance, confession and baptism.

Acts 10:44-48
While Peter was still speaking these words, the Holy Spirit fell upon all those who heard the word. And those of the circumcision who believed were astonished, as many as came with Peter, because the gift of the Holy Spirit had been poured out on the Gentiles also. For

they heard them speak with tongues and magnify God. Then Peter answered "Can anyone forbid water, that these should not be baptized who have received the Holy Spirit just as we have?" And he commanded them to be baptized in the name of the Lord. Then they asked him to stay a few days.

I think it is important to think about why Peter is saying this. He is telling the event in a way that allows us to see that this is something special that God was doing to show acceptance of the Gentiles.

Act 10:46-47

For they heard them speak with tongues and magnify God. Then Peter answered "Can anyone forbid water, that these should not be baptized who have received the Holy Spirit just as we have?" And he commanded them to be baptized in the name of the Lord. Then they asked him to stay a few days.

This verse implies that those of the circumcision would have refused to let them be baptized into Christ and thus put on Christ, if this miracle had not taken place to show that God did indeed accept the Gentiles. If we understand that the scripture teaches that we need to be baptized into Christ, to be put into Christ, we can see the significance of this verse. The Jews would have refused to let the Gentiles enter into the Body of Christ, which is the same as saying the Jews would have refused to allow them to be saved. This is the reason that the Holy Spirit was poured out on them prior to their knowledge of Jesus Christ and their opportunity to respond to the gospel.

> *And he commanded them to be baptized in the name of the Lord. Then they asked him to stay a few days.*

There is no mention of a sinner's prayer or anyone asking Jesus into their heart. What we do find is they believed and are commanded to be baptized. This is consistent and true to all other accounts of Biblical salvation, as recorded by the apostles who were guided by the Holy Spirit.

Now let's follow up with Peter's retelling of the events.

> *Acts 11:14-18*
> *...who will tell you words by which you and all your household will be saved.' And as I began to speak, the Holy Spirit fell upon them, as upon us at the beginning. Then I remembered the word of the Lord, how He said, 'John indeed baptized with water, but you shall be baptized with the Holy Spirit.' If therefore God gave them the same gift as He gave us when we believed on the Lord Jesus Christ, who was I that I could withstand God?" When they heard these things they became silent; and they glorified God, saying, "Then God has also granted to the Gentiles repentance to life."*

I think that it is important to reflect on why Peter is saying this, that this is something that has never before happened. He is telling the event in a way that allows us to see that this is something special that God was doing to show acceptance to the Gentiles. Verse fourteen also makes it clear that they did not know what to do to receive salvation and that Peter's purpose in coming to them was to preach the gospel message of Jesus Christ to them so they might understand and be saved. Please notice in verse fifteen, Peter clearly says, *As I began to speak,* clearly showing that Cornelius and the rest of the Gentiles had the Holy Spirit fall upon them prior to their ability to believe (because they had not heard), repent (what would they repent of?), confess (we cannot confess that which we do not know), and baptism/immersion in water. We also clearly see from these two accounts that after they were given an opportunity to hear the message, they acted in obedience to that message by being baptized/ immersed straightaway in water.

Verses seventeen and eighteen help us to clearly understand the purpose of God pouring out the Holy Spirit upon the Gentile, Cornelius, and this household:

> *Then I remembered the word of the Lord, how He said, 'John indeed baptized with water, but you shall be baptized with the Holy Spirit.' If therefore God gave them the same gift as He gave us when we believed on the Lord Jesus Christ, who was I that I could withstand God?" When they heard these things they became silent; and they glorified God, saying, "Then God has also granted to the Gentiles repentance to life."*

It was a miracle to proclaim to the world that God considered the Gentiles eligible for the Kingdom of God. My hope is that by breaking down the above passages, the purpose of the outpouring of the Holy

Spirit prior to faith/belief, repentance, confession, and immersion/baptism becomes simple and evident. We can now look at Cornelius' conversion and understand that he was not saved prior to his belief or immersion/baptism into Jesus Christ.

The book of Acts is full of example after example of people being saved and we see the same pattern throughout the entire book, with Cornelius being the only exception. Because of the significance of Gentiles now being able to be a part of the accepted people of God, a miracle of the Holy Spirit being poured out prior to belief, repentance or baptism is done by God. By outpouring His Spirit on the heathen Gentiles, He ends all possible arguments by the Jews that the Gentiles are unclean and unable to receive salvation. Who can stand against the Spirit of God? The scriptural accounts of people being saved are the same throughout Acts: an individual hears and is pricked to the heart, believes the message of salvation, they repent, confess Jesus as Christ, and are baptized right away into Jesus Christ's death (even at midnight). We see that the instruction is then to live with a heart turned towards God and obey His words. All of the above works together to bring us into Christ. To leave out any part of what God has clearly outlined in His Word is to rebel against God and His instructions and to make one passage in the word of God contradict or void out other passages.

Psalm 119:160
The entirety of Your word is truth,
And every one of Your righteous judgments endures forever.

Matthew 4:4
But He answered and said, "It is written, 'Man shall
not live by bread alone, but by every word that proceeds
from the mouth of God.'"

The last objection that we will look at is found in Mark
chapter 16:15-16 Let's read it together and then closely
consider what is being said.

Mark 16:15-16
And He said to them, "Go into all the world and
preach the gospel to every creature. He who believes and
is baptized will be saved; but he who does not believe
will be condemned.

Whenever this passage is quoted as proof that belief and
baptism are both required for salvation, the rebuttal is,
"But it doesn't say, *'he who does not believe and is not baptized*
will be condemned.'" This is not a logical argument. We
clearly see this if we just change the wording into
something practical from everyday life. For example...I
say, "Friend, if you go to the store and buy bread, I will
give you a million dollars. If you do not go to the store,
I will not give you a million dollars." I do not need to
say, "If you do not go to the store and do not buy
bread." Logically that is implied. If you do not go to the
store, you cannot buy bread. The same is equally true of
Mark 16:16; if you do not believe, you will not be
baptized. To think that one would be baptized for no
reason is ridiculous, and more importantly, jumping into
a pool of water has never saved anyone without the

belief that this is a burial into the death of their Savior. It is a given and logically implied in the statement.

Speaking of objections, I think it would be good to remember that

Belief **alone** does not save us. The demons believe and tremble.

James 2:19

You believe that there is one God. You do well. Even the demons believe—and tremble!

Confession **alone** does not save us, even the demons confess Jesus as God.

Luke 4:34
...saying, "Let us alone! What have we to do with You, Jesus of Nazareth? Did You come to destroy us? I know who You are—the Holy One of God!"

I think that we can agree that no demon is saved, yet the scripture clearly tells us that demons believe and confess Jesus as Christ. We can see by this that belief alone or confession alone does not save us. Repentance alone has saved no one, and neither has baptism (people immerse themselves in water all the time). God's word shows us that it is the working together of all these commands (Repent, confess, believe, be baptized, and walk in love and obedience to Christ) that brings us to Christ and presents us faultless before the Father.

To sum up, baptism plays a part in individuals being born again, put into Christ, or saved. I believe that the scripture is very clear that Faith, Belief, Confession, and Baptism are the recipe for Salvation. Just like you would not leave out flour or any other ingredient for cookies and still call them cookies, God indeed shows us a recipe for Salvation. To ignore or downplay the importance of His key ingredients is to be disobedient to what He has commanded. It also sadly gives assurance of salvation to individuals who have not yet been washed of their sins and have not been put into Christ so that they can rise with Him (Rom. 6; Col. 3; Gal. 3:27; Col. 2:12). We are declaring people to be saved and in Christ when they believe, yet The Word (Jesus Christ) declares them to be saved when they have obeyed all of what He has commanded (repent, confess, believe, be baptized, and walk in love and obedience to Christ).

I truly hope that this look at possible objections has helped you see that God's Word does not contradict itself. Throughout the entire Bible, there is the same and consistent message declaring how we are put into Christ, saved and our sins forgiven.

H. Roye

PART 4

A Quick Review

Let's take a minute for a quick review. The following is the process by which we are saved as seen in God's Word.

We must hear...

We must hear the good news, that Jesus Christ came into the world to save ALL that would love and obey Him. He lived a perfect life, died an unspeakable death, and was raised to live again, showing His mastery over death. We now have hope that we too may have the victory over death.

Romans 10:17
So then faith comes by hearing, and hearing by the word of God.

1 Corinthians 1:21
For since, in the wisdom of God, the world through wisdom did not know God, it pleased God through the foolishness of the message preached to save those who believe.

163

We must have faith and believe...

Hebrews 11:6
But without faith it is impossible to please Him, for he who comes to God must believe that He is, and that He is a rewarder of those that diligently seek Him.

Mark 16:15-16
And He said to them, "Go into all the world and preach the gospel to every creature. He who believes and is baptized will be saved; but he who does not believe will be condemned.

John 8:24
Therefore I said to you that you will die in your sins; for if you do not believe that I am He, you will die in your sins."

Faith and belief alone do not save us, because even Satan and the demons believe. Yet their belief does not save them, nor put them into a saving relationship with Jesus Christ.

James 2:19
You believe that there is one God. You do well. Even the demons believe—and tremble!

We must repent...

Acts 2:38
Then Peter said to them, "Repent, and let every one of you be baptized in the name of Jesus Christ for the

remission of sins; and you shall receive the gift of the Holy Spirit.

2 Peter 3:9
The Lord is not slack concerning His promise, as some men count slackness, but is longsuffering toward us, not willing that any should perish, but that all should come to repentance.

Acts 17:30
Truly, these times of ignorance God overlooked, but now commands all men everywhere to repent.

Luke 13:3
I tell you, no; but unless you repent you will all likewise perish.

Repenting is defined in God's Word as a complete turning away from sin and walking towards God, the truth and righteousness.

We must confess...

Matthew 10:32-33
Therefore whoever confesses Me before men, him I will also confess before My Father who is in heaven. But whoever denies Me before men, him I will also deny before My Father who is in heaven.

Romans 10:10
For with the heart one believes unto righteousness, and with the mouth confession is made unto salvation.

Acts 8:36-37
Now as they went down the road, they came to some
water. And the eunuch said, "See, here is water. What
hinders me from being baptized?" Then Philip said, "If
you believe with all your heart, you may." And he
answered and said, "I believe that Jesus Christ is the
Son of God."

Confession alone does not save us, since even the demons confess Jesus, as mentioned earlier. But a willingness to confess and openly align yourself with your Savior and His truths is a vital step in our coming to Jesus Christ. (Luke 4:34)

We must be baptized/immersed in water...

We cannot escape the fact that if we are not baptized into Christ, we will not be raised with Christ, and the old man is not put to death! So to preach salvation to someone and leave out baptism is to give them a false hope of salvation, because they have neither been washed of their sins or buried with Christ so that they can be raised up with Him! Satan rejoices when men leave out baptism as part of God's plan for salvation. As in the Garden of Eden, Satan spoke most of the truth, he cleverly added just one word. The result was physical and spiritual death.

Galatians 3:27
For as many of you as have been baptized into Christ
have put on Christ.

Galatians reaffirms that we put on Christ when we are baptized/immersed into His death. It fits perfectly with Romans 6.

2 Corinthians 5:17
Therefore if anyone is in Christ, he is a new creation: old things have passed away; behold, all things have become new.

This backs up Romans 6 and causes us to reflect and ask ourselves am I *In Christ?* Because only *In Christ* do we become a new creation and do the old things pass away.

1 Peter 3:20-21
…who formerly were disobedient, when once the Divine longsuffering waited in the days of Noah, while the ark was being prepared, in which a few, that is, eight souls, were saved through water. There is also an antitype which now saves us - baptism (not the removal of the filth of the flesh, but the answer of a good conscience toward God), through the resurrection of Jesus Christ.

I love how God's word is consistent from Genesis to Revelation. The account of Noah is a foreshadowing. There is only one door. When God shuts the door, the eight souls are saved because they believed and got into the ark.

Mark 16:15-16
And He said to them, "Go into all the world and preach the gospel to every creature. He who believes and

is baptized will be saved; but he who does not believe will be condemned.

Acts 10:48
And he commanded them to be baptized in the name of the Lord. Then they asked him to stay a few days.

Matthew 28:19
Go therefore and make disciples of all the nations, baptizing them in the name of the Father and of the Son and of the Holy Spirit.

Acts 2:38
Then Peter said unto them, "Repent, and let every one of you be baptized in the name of Jesus Christ for the remission of sins; and you shall receive the gift of the Holy Spirit."

It is important to point out that we are to be baptized for the forgiveness of our sins and then we are promised the gift of the Holy Spirit. This is the biblical pattern.

To sum up, when a person is baptized, they are born again, put into Christ, clothed in Christ and saved. I believe that the scripture is very clear that Faith, Belief, Confession, and Baptism are God's recipe for Salvation. God has shown us a recipe for Salvation and to ignore or downplay the importance of His key ingredients, is to be disobedient to what He has commanded. Sadly, it gives a false assurance of salvation to individuals who have not as yet been washed of their sins and have not been put into Christ so that they can be raised with Him.

Remain Faithful...

Finally, we must remain faithful! This is another area where John Calvin and "once saved, always saved" doctrines have led many into a false belief that is not found in the Word of God. There are hundreds of scriptures from Genesis to Revelation that completely contradict these doctrines. Let's look again at the first and the last ones together. Again, I would implore you to examine the rest of the scripture diligently yourself.

Genesis 4:6-7
So the LORD said to Cain, "Why are you angry? And why has your countenance fallen? If you do well, will you not be accepted? And if you do not do well, sin lies at the door. And its desire is for you, but you should rule over it."

What does God say to Cain? He tells him to DO well and he will be accepted. But if he does NOT DO well, he will not. He goes on further to implore him to choose right and master the sin. Let's go on to Revelation 20:12.

And I saw the dead, small and great, stand before God, and books were opened. And another book was opened, which is the Book of Life. And the dead were judged according to their works, by the things which were written in the books.

Please note that the dead were judged according to their works. Again, these verses do not stand alone as there are hundreds of verses that say the same thing. Please follow the exhortation in 2 Tim. 2:15 and study them. I tried to use scriptures from the Old Testament and the New Testament because God is consistent and does not contradict Himself.

The following verse are extremely important because God defines the term of election/chosen/predestined. God does not need our help in defining or explaining concepts found in His Word. The Bible, His Word, always defines within itself. This verse in Acts could not be more direct in conveying the idea that God accepts/chooses those that fear Him and work righteousness.

Acts 10:34-35
Then Peter opened his mouth, and said: "In truth I perceive that God shows no partiality. But in every nation whoever fears Him and works righteousness is accepted by Him."

Matthew 24:13
But he who endures to the end shall be saved.

Titus 2:11-14
For the grace of God that brings salvation has appeared to all men, teaching us that, denying ungodliness and worldly lusts, we should live soberly, righteously, and godly in the present age, looking for the blessed hope and glorious appearing of our great God and Savior Jesus Christ, who gave Himself for us, that He might redeem us from every lawless deed and purify for Himself His own special people, zealous for good works.

Titus 3:5-8

Not by works of righteousness which we have done, but according to His mercy He saved us, through the washing of regeneration and renewing of the Holy Spirit, whom He poured out on us abundantly through Jesus Christ our Savior, that having been justified by His grace we should become heirs according to the hope of eternal life. This is a faithful saying, and these things I want you to affirm constantly, that those who have believed in God should be careful to maintain good works. These things are good and profitable to men.

Let's not fail to notice how the above verses clarify the difference between the works of righteousness/works of the law and the admonishment to maintain good works. Clearly bringing to our attention that we were not saved by the works of the law but by Christ's blood alone we are washed and clothed in Him. We are even told specifically that He saved us by the washing of regeneration and the renewing of the Holy Spirit. Remember again that we see this exact pattern in the first gospel sermon in Acts 2:38. First, we are washed/immersed then we receive the gift of the Holy Spirit.

Here are some more great verses where God defines His elect or chosen people.

I love that God doesn't leave us to flounder and guess what He means, He defines for us what He intends for us to understand about who His chosen people are.

As defined in the following verses.
1 Samuel 12:24
2 Chronicles 15:9
Nehemiah 9:29
Psalms 31:19-20; 31:23-24; 37:37-40; 50:23
Ecclesiastes 12:13-14
Isaiah 66:2
Micah 6:6-8
Matthew 3:10; 12:50; 20:16; 22:2-14; 24:13; 25:34-36
Mark 13:13
Luke 8:12-15; 8:21; 10:25-28
John 1:10-13; 3:17-21; 4:23; 8:24 & 51; 10:9; 15:1-17
Acts 2:47
Romans 2:7-10
2 Thessalonians 2:10-15
1 Timothy 4:16
Hebrews 5:8-9; 5:12-15
1 Peter 1:2
2 Peter 1:10
1 John 2:29

Of course, there are many more, but I love these and believe they will give you a great foundation.

Now, verses on remaining faithful, because we can fall if we choose....

Proverbs 28:9
One who turns away his ear from hearing the law, even his prayer is an abomination.

Hebrews 10:26-39

For if we sin willfully after we have received the knowledge of the truth, there no longer remains a sacrifice for sins, but a certain fearful expectation of judgment, and fiery indignation which will devour the adversaries. Anyone who has rejected Moses' law dies without mercy on the testimony of two or three witnesses. Of how much worse punishment, do you suppose, will he be thought worthy who has trampled the Son of God underfoot, counted the blood of the covenant by which he was sanctified a common thing, and insulted the Spirit of grace? For we know Him who said, "Vengeance is Mine, I will repay," says the Lord. And again, "The Lord will judge His people." It is a fearful thing to fall into the hands of the living God. But recall the former days in which, after you were illuminated, you endured a great struggle with sufferings: partly while you were made a spectacle both by reproaches and tribulations, and partly while you became companions of those who were so treated; for you had compassion on me in my chains, and joyfully accepted the plundering of your goods, knowing that you have a better and an enduring possession for yourselves in heaven. Therefore do not cast away your confidence, which has great reward. For you have need of endurance, so that after you have done the will of God, you may receive the promise:

For yet a little while,
And He who is coming will come and will not tarry.
Now the just shall live by faith;
But if anyone draws back,
My soul has no pleasure in him."
But we are not of those who draw back to perdition, but of those who believe to the saving of the soul.

Please pay close attention as this passage states that you can lose your salvation at least four times very clearly.

Hebrews 12:15
Looking carefully lest anyone fall short of the grace of God; lest any root of bitterness springing up cause trouble, and by this many become defiled.

Please note here the phrase *fall short of the grace of God.* Remember we are revisiting these verses to show that God's word does not teach *once saved always saved.* We choose daily to walk towards God and righteousness, or we choose to walk away.

Romans 11:11-24
I say then, have they stumbled that they should fall? Certainly not! But through their fall, to provoke them to jealousy, salvation has come to the Gentiles. Now if their fall is riches for the world, and their failure riches for the Gentiles, how much more their fullness! For I speak to you Gentiles; inasmuch as I am an apostle to the Gentiles, I magnify my ministry, if by any means I may provoke to jealousy those who are my flesh and save some of them. For if their being cast away is the reconciling of the world, what will their acceptance be but life from the dead? For if the first fruit is holy, the lump is also holy; and if the root is holy, so are the branches. And if some of the branches were broken off, and you, being a wild olive tree, were grafted in among them, and with them became a partaker of the root and fatness of the olive tree, do not boast against the branches. But if you do boast, remember that you do not

support the root, but the root supports you. You will say then, "Branches were broken off that I might be grafted in." Well said. Because of unbelief they were broken off, and you stand by faith. Do not be haughty, but fear. For if God did not spare the natural branches, He may not spare you either. Therefore consider the goodness and severity of God: on those who fell, severity; but toward you, goodness, if you continue in His goodness. Otherwise you also will be cut off. And they also, if they do not continue in unbelief, will be grafted in, for God is able to graft them in again. For if you were cut out of the olive tree which is wild by nature, and were grafted contrary to nature into a cultivated olive tree, how much more will these, who are natural branches, be grafted into their own olive tree?

Again, we see that we can be cast away after being grafted in!

Ezekiel 18:1-32
The word of the Lord came to me again, saying, "What do you mean when you use this proverb concerning the land of Israel, saying:
'The fathers have eaten sour grapes, and the children's teeth are set on edge'?
"As I live," says the Lord God, "you shall no longer use this proverb in Israel.
Behold, all souls are Mine;
The soul of the father
As well as the soul of the son is Mine;
The soul who sins shall die.

But if a man is just
And does what is lawful and right;
If he has not eaten on the mountains,
Nor lifted up his eyes to the idols of the house of Israel,
Nor defiled his neighbor's wife,
Nor approached a woman during her impurity;
If he has not oppressed anyone,
But has given his bread to the hungry
And covered the naked with clothing;
If he has not exacted usury
Nor taken any increase,
But has withdrawn his hand from iniquity
And executed true judgment between man and man;
And kept My judgments faithfully-
He is just;
He shall surely live!"
Says the Lord God.
If he begets a son who is a robber
Or as shedder of blood,
Who does any of these things
And does none of those duties,
But has eaten on the mountains
Or defiled his neighbor's wife;
If he has oppressed the poor and needy,
Robbed by violence,
Not restored the pledge,
Lifted his eyes to the idols,
Or committed abomination;
If he has exacted usury
Or taken increase —
Shall he live then?
He shall not live!
If he has done any of these abominations,

He shall surely die;
His blood shall be upon him.
If, however, he begets a son
Who sees all the sins which his father has done,
Who has not eaten on the mountains,
Nor lifted his eyes to the idols of the house of Israel,
Nor defiled his neighbor's wife;
Has not oppressed anyone,
Nor withheld a pledge,
Nor robbed by violence,
But has given his bread to the hungry
And covered the naked with clothing;
Who has withdrawn his hand from the poor
And not received usury or increase,
But has executed My judgments
And walked in My statutes-
He shall not die for the iniquity of his father;
He shall surely live!
As for his father,
Because he cruelly oppressed,
Robbed his brother by violence,
And did what is not good among his people,
Behold, he shall die for his iniquity.
Yet you say, 'Why should the son not bear the guilt of the father?' Because the son has done what is lawful and right, and has kept all My statutes and observed them, he shall surely live. The soul who sins shall die. The son shall not bear the guilt of the father, nor the father bear the guilt of the son. The righteousness of the righteous shall be upon himself, and the wickedness of the wicked shall be upon himself. But if a wicked man turns from all his sins which he has committed, keeps all My statutes, and does what is lawful and right, he shall

surely live; he shall not die. None of the transgressions which he has committed shall be remembered against him; because of the righteousness which he has done, he shall live. Do I have any pleasure at all that the wicked should die?" says the Lord God, "and not that he should turn from his ways and live? But when a righteous man turns away from his righteousness and commits iniquity, and does according to all the abominations that the wicked man does, shall he live? All the righteousness which he has done shall not be remembered; because of the unfaithfulness of which he is guilty and the sin which he has committed, because of them he shall die. Yet you say, 'The way of the Lord is not fair.' Hear now, O house of Israel, is it not My way which is fair, and your ways which are not fair? When a righteous man turns away from his righteousness, commits iniquity, and dies in it, it is because of the iniquity which he has done that he dies. Again, when a wicked man turns away from the wickedness which he committed, and does what is lawful and right, he preserves himself alive. Because he considers and turns away from all the transgressions which he committed, he shall surely live; he shall not die. Yet the house of Israel says, 'The way of the Lord is not fair.' O house of Israel, is it not My ways which are fair, and your ways which are not fair? Therefore I will judge you, O house of Israel, every one according to his ways," says the Lord God. "Repent, and turn from all your transgressions, so that iniquity will not be your ruin. Cast away from you all the transgressions which you have committed, and get yourselves a new heart and a new spirit. For why should you die, O house of Israel? For I have no pleasure in the death of one who dies," says the Lord God. "Therefore turn and live!"

If you are thinking, "Well, that is the Old Testament", consider that God has not changed, as He presented the same thoughts in the book of John.

John 15:1-27

I am the true vine, and my Father is the vinedresser. Every branch in Me that does not bear fruit He takes away; and every branch that bears fruit He prunes, that it may bear more fruit. You are already clean because of the word which I have spoken to you. Abide in Me, and I in you. As the branch cannot bear fruit of itself, unless it abides in the vine, neither can you, unless you abide in Me. I am the vine, you are the branches. He who abides in Me, and I in him, bears much fruit; for without Me you can do nothing. If anyone does not abide in Me, he is cast out as a branch and is withered; and they gather them and throw them into the fire, and they are burned. If you abide in Me, and My words abide in you, you will ask what you desire, and it shall be done for you. By this My Father is glorified, that you bear much fruit; so you will be My disciples. As the Father loved me, I also have loved you; abide in My love, just as I have kept My Father's commandments and abide in His love. These things I have spoken to you, that My joy may remain in you, and that your joy may be full. This is My commandment, that you love one another as I have loved you. Greater love has no one than this, than to lay down one's life for his friends. You are My friends if you do whatever I command you. No longer do I call you servants, for a servant does not know what his *master is doing; but I have called you friends, for all things that I heard from My Father I have made known to you. You did not choose Me, but I chose you and appointed you that you should go and bear fruit, and that your fruit should remain, that whatever you ask the Father in My name He may give you. These things I command you, that you love one another. If the world hates you, you know that it hated Me before it hated you. If you were of the world, the world would love its own. Yet because you are not of the world, but I chose you out of the world, therefore the world hates you. Remember the word that I said to you, 'A servant is not greater than his master.' If they persecuted Me, they will also persecute you. If they kept My word, they will keep yours also. But all these things they will do to you for My name's sake, because they do not know Him who sent Me. <u>If I had not come and spoken to them, they would have no sin, but now they have no excuse for their sin.</u> He who hates Me hates My Father also. If I had not done among them the works which no one else did, they would have no sin; but now they have seen and also hated both Me and My Father. But this happened that the word might be fulfilled which is written in their law, 'They hated Me without a cause.' But when the Helper comes, whom I shall send to you from the Father, the Spirit of truth who proceeds from the Father, He will testify of Me. And you will bear witness, because you have been with me from the beginning.*

The above verses show that we must remain faithful to God in order to be saved.

Here is a little more reading to further establish the above verses.

Genesis 4:6-7
Deuteronomy 30:15-19
2 Chronicles 7:14-20; 12:12; 12:14
Jeremiah 7:23
Ezekiel 3:20-21; 18
Matthew 25:1-30
Luke 8:12-15; 9:62; 12:41-46; 14:34
John 8:31; 15:1-6
Acts 4:32; 5:1-11; 13:43-46; 14:22; 20:28-32
Romans 11:11-24
1 Corinthians 8:11-12; 9:26-27; 10:1-14; 15:58
Galatians 5:1-4; 6:1
Colossians 1:21-23
1 Timothy 1:18-21; 3:6-7; 4:1; 5:8; 6:10; 6:20-21
2 Timothy 2:9-10; 2:16-18
Hebrews 3:6, 12, 14; 4:1-2 & 11; 6:4-8; 12:15
James 5:12, 19-20
1 Peter 5:8-9
2 Peter 2:1, 14, 20-22; 3:17
I John 1:5-10
2 John 2:8-9
Revelation 2:4-5; 3:4-6, 16-22

Why is there a lack of zeal in the Church of God? Well, recently I heard a minister say that your salvation was like taking a class in which at the beginning of the class, you are told that you will receive an "A" no matter what you do. This was his analogy for the Christian walk. I felt like crying upon hearing this. We all know that this has actually been done by professors and the results are horrible. Nobody does anything. This is human nature. If we use the Bible, God's Word, for the analogy, it would go like this.....You are invited to join a class, but to remain in the class, you must come as often as possible, do your best on the homework and tests, and tell others about what you are learning. Everyone who does this will receive an "A".

Again, there are hundreds of scriptures that refute Calvinism and the *'once saved always saved'* doctrine. At their very foundation, these doctrines state unequivocally that you do not have free will, and that God makes all the decisions for you. Calvinists are taught *'once saved always saved'* from the point of salvation (that is why there is nothing you can do to fall from grace, you must remain saved once saved).

It seems we have a contradiction, because the Bible clearly says that...

Jude 1:24
Now to him who is able to keep you from stumbling,
And to present you faultless
Before the presence of His glory with exceeding joy...

Let's remember to always let God define His words by His words.

Here is the verse that defines how Jesus is able to keep us from falling. Remember, Jesus is the Word.

John 1:1-4

In the beginning was the Word, and the Word was with God, and the Word was God. He was in the beginning with God. All things were made through him, and without Him nothing was made that was made. In Him was life, and the life was the light of men.

Jesus is literally the Bible you hold in your hands. If we obey the word and implant it into our hearts and minds, the promise of 2 Peter 1:10 is what we can trust in. This is how Jesus keeps us from falling as defined by Him.

2 Peter 1:4-12

By which have been given to us exceedingly great and precious promises, that through these you may be partakers of the divine nature, having escaped the corruption that is in the world through lust. But also for this very reason, giving all diligence, add to your faith virtue, to virtue knowledge, to knowledge self-control, to self-control perseverance, to perseverance godliness, to godliness brotherly kindness, and to brotherly kindness love. For if these things are yours and abound, you will be neither barren nor unfruitful in the knowledge of our Lord Jesus Christ. For he who lacks these things is shortsighted, even to blindness, and has forgotten that he was cleansed from his old sins. Therefore, brethren, be even more diligent to make your call and election sure, for if you do these things you will never stumble; for so an entrance will be supplied to you abundantly into the everlasting kingdom of our Lord and Savior Jesus Christ. Wherefore I will not be negligent to put you always in remembrance of these things, though ye know them, and be established in the present truth.

Let's focus on verses 10-11 (underlined above) for a minute, so we don't miss out on God's important truth. If we wish to make our calling and election sure, if we wish to never fall, we are to give diligence to do these things! Well, what things? The things we were just told to do in verses 4-8.

Give all diligence to add to your faith.....
Virtue
Knowledge
Temperance
Patience
Godliness
Brotherly Kindness
LOVE
Let these above things be in you and abound.
(2 Peter 1:4-8)

The first two verses of Romans Chapter 8 sum up very nicely and tie together some of these important concepts that we have been examining. Romans points out that if we are *in Christ Jesus* we are no longer under condemnation. Next, we are pointed to the Law of the Spirit of Life which again is *in Christ Jesus* and told how this law has freed us from the law of sin and death. As always God's word fits perfectly together Romans with Galatians chapter 3.

Romans 8:1-2
There is therefore now no condemnation to them

which are in Christ Jesus, who walk not after the flesh, but after the Spirit. For the law of the Spirit of life in Christ Jesus hath made me free from the law of sin and death.

Our role being clear we are to remain faithful until death.

Revelation 2:10
Do not fear any of those things which you are about to suffer. Indeed, the devil is about to throw some of you into prison, that you may be tested, and you will have tribulation ten days. Be faithful until death, and I will give you a crown of life.

A few more verses on how we are kept from falling.

Psalm 37:3
John 15:1-17
Acts 20:23
Galatians 5:16
2 Timothy 3:12-17
James 1:2-4
1 Peter 1:5
1 John 1:5-10
1 John 2:24-25, 28

God does not want us to be confused about how our actions bear witness to our faith. Our works demonstrate whom we love and serve. (Please, read the books of James and 1 John, and chapter 15 of the gospel of John) These passages clearly draw for us the same picture we find in Romans.

Romans 6:16
Do you not know that to whom you present yourselves
slaves to obey, you are that one's slaves whom you obey,
whether of sin leading to death, or of obedience leading
to righteousness?

To sum up the gospel plan of salvation:

HEAR

BELIEVE AND HAVE FAITH

REPENT OF SIN AND TURN TOWARDS GOD

CONFESS

BE IMMERSED IN WATER/ BAPTIZED

AND LIVE FAITHFULLY AS BLOOD-BOUGHT
SERVANTS OF JESUS CHRIST

Acts 17:11
These were more fair-minded than those in
Thessalonica, in that they received the word with all
readiness, and searched the Scriptures daily to find out
whether these things were so.

Jesus Invites You!

Matthew 11:28-30
*Come to Me, all you who labor and are heavy laden,
and I will give you rest. Take My yoke upon you and
learn from Me, for I am gentle and lowly in heart, and
you will find rest for your souls. For My yoke is easy
and My burden is light.*

Matthew 19:16-21
*Now behold, one came and said to him, "Good
Teacher, what good thing shall I do, that I may have
eternal life?" So He said to him, "Why do you call Me
good? No one is good but One, that is, God. But if you
want to enter into life, keep the commandments." He
said to Him, "Which ones?" Jesus said, "'You shall
not murder,' 'You shall not commit adultery,' 'You
shall not steal,' 'You shall not bear false witness,'
'Honor your father and your mother,' and, 'You shall
love your neighbor as yourself.'" The young man said to
Him, "All these things I have kept from my youth.
What do I still lack?" Jesus said to him, "If you want
to be perfect, go, sell what you have and give to the poor,
and you will have treasure in heaven; and come, follow
Me."*

Jesus held out His loving hand and gave the rich young
ruler an invitation.
Likewise, Jesus has presented you with an invitation to
follow Him. Just as with the rich young ruler, He has
told you to do something if you "want to enter into life."

Jesus has asked that you...

HEAR

BELIEVE AND HAVE FAITH

REPENT OF SIN AND TURN TOWARDS GOD

CONFESS

BE IMMERSED IN WATER/ BAPTIZED

AND LIVE FAITHFULLY AS BLOOD-BOUGHT SERVANTS OF JESUS CHRIST.

The question, my friend, is will you walk away sorrowful, unwilling to obey His conditions? Or will you obey from the heart and enter into life and be clothed *IN HIM?*

His Promises to Those Who Are IN HIM

We have clearly seen through God's Word what it means to be "*IN HIM*" as defined by God in His Word. It is a tremendously blessed and wonderful condition to be found *in Christ*. Remember, these promises are to those who have been buried with our Lord in baptism, thus clothing themselves in Jesus Christ and His blood. Let's take a peek at some of those blessings for those that are *IN HIM*.

Romans 3:24
Being justified freely by His grace through the redemption that is in Christ Jesus.

Romans 8:1-2
There is therefore now no condemnation to those who are in Christ Jesus, who do not walk according to the flesh, but according to the Spirit. For the law of the Spirit of life in Christ Jesus has made me free from the law of sin and death.

Romans 12:5
So we, being many, are one body in Christ, and individually members of one another.

1 Corinthians 1:2
To the church of God which is at Corinth, to those who are sanctified in Christ Jesus, called to be saints, with all who in every place call on the name of Jesus Christ our Lord, both theirs and ours.

1 Corinthians 1:30
But of him you are in Christ Jesus, who became for us wisdom from God – and righteousness and sanctification and redemption.

1 Corinthians 15:22
For as in Adam all die, even so in Christ shall all be made alive.

2 Cor 1:21
Now He who establishes us with you in Christ and has anointed us is God.

2 Corinthians 2:14
Now thanks be to God who always leads us in triumph in Christ, and through us diffuses the fragrance of His knowledge in every place.

2 Corinthians 3:14
But their minds were blinded. For until this day the same veil remains unlifted in the reading of the Old Testament, because the veil is taken away in Christ.

2 Corinthians 5:17
Therefore, if anyone is in Christ, he is a new creation; old things have passed away; behold, all things have become new.

2 Corinthians 5:19
That is, that God was in Christ reconciling the world to Himself, not imputing their trespasses to them, and has committed to us the word of reconciliation.

Colossians 1:28
Him we preach, warning every man and teaching every man in all wisdom, that we may present every man perfect in Christ Jesus.

1 Thessalonians 4:16
For this we say to you by the word of the Lord, that we who are alive and remain until the coming of the Lord will by no means precede those who are asleep.

1 Thessalonians 5:18
In everything give thanks; for this is the will of God in Christ Jesus for you.

1 Timothy 1:14
And the grace of our Lord was exceeding abundant, with faith and love which are in Christ Jesus.

2 Timothy 1:9
Who has saved us and called us with a holy calling, not according to our works, but according to His own purpose and grace which has given to us in Christ Jesus before time began.

2 Timothy 1:13
Hold fast the pattern of sound words which you have heard from me, in faith and love which are in Christ Jesus.

2 Timothy 2:1
You therefore, my son, be strong in the grace that is in Christ Jesus.

2 Timothy 2:10
Therefore I endure all things for the sake of the elect, that they also may obtain the salvation which is in Christ Jesus with eternal glory.

2 Timothy 3:15
And that from childhood you have known the Holy Scriptures, which are able to make you wise for salvation through faith which is in Christ Jesus.

Philemon 1:6
That the sharing of your faith may become effective by the acknowledgement of every good thing which is in you in Christ Jesus.

2 Peter 1:8
For if these things are yours and abound, you will be neither barren nor unfruitful in the knowledge of our Lord Jesus Christ.

2 John 1:9

Whoever transgresses and does not abide in the doctrine of Christ does not have God. He who abides in the doctrine of Christ has both the Father and the Son.

Acts 17:28

For in him we live and move and have our being, as also some of your own poets have said, 'For we are also His offspring.'

John 1:4

In Him was life; and the life was the light of men.

John 3:15-16

That whoever believes in Him should not perish but have eternal life. For God so loved the world that He gave His only begotten Son, that whoever believes in Him should not perish but have everlasting life.

2 Corinthians 1:20

For all the promises of God in Him are Yes, and in Him Amen, to the glory of God through us.

2 Corinthians 5:21

For he made Him who knew no sin to be sin for us, that we might become the righteousness of God in Him.

Ephesians 1:4

Just as He chose us in Him before the foundation of the world, that we should be holy and without blame before Him in love.

Ephesians 1:10
That in the dispensation of the fulness of the times He might gather together in one all things in Christ, both which are in heaven, and which are on earth – in Him.

Philippians 3:9
And be found in Him, not having my own righteousness, which is from the law, but that which is through faith in Christ, the righteousness which is from God by faith.

Colossians 2:6-7
As you therefore have received Christ Jesus the Lord, so walk in Him, rooted and built up in Him and established in the faith, as you have been taught, abounding in it with thanksgiving.

Colossians 2:10
And you are complete in Him, who is the head of all principality and power.

1 John 2:5-6
But whoever keeps His word, truly the love of God is perfected in him. By this we know that we are in Him. He who says he abides in Him ought himself also to walk just as He walked.

1 John 2:8
Again, a new commandment I write to you, which thing is true in Him and in you, because the darkness is passing away, the true light is already shining.

1 John 2:27
But the anointing which you have received from Him abides in you, and you do not need that anyone teach you; but as the same anointing teaches you concerning all things, and is true, and is not a lie, and just as it has taught you, you will abide in Him.

1 John 3:5-6
And you know that He was manifested to take away our sins, and in Him there is no sin. Whoever abides in Him does not sin. Whoever sins has neither seen Him nor known Him.

1 John 3:24
Now he who keeps His commandments abides in Him, and He in him. And by this we know that He abides in us, by the Spirit whom He has given us.

1 John 4:13
By this we know that we abide in Him, and He in us, because He has given us of His Spirit.

1 John 5:14-15
Now this is the confidence that we have in Him, that if we ask anything according to His will, He hears us. And if we know that He hears us, whatever we ask, we know that we have the petitions that we have asked of Him.

1 John 5:20
And we know that the Son of God has come and has given us an understanding, that we may know Him who

is true; and we are in Him who is true, in His Son Jesus Christ. This is the true God, and eternal life.

Ephesians 1:6
To the praise of the glory of His grace, by which He made us accepted in the Beloved.

Eph 6:10
Finally, my brethren, be strong in the Lord, and in the power of His might.

Ephesians 1:7
In Him we have redemption through His blood, the forgiveness of sins, according to the riches of His grace.

Ephesians 1:11

In Him also we have obtained an inheritance, being predestined according to the purpose of Him who works all things according to the counsel of His will.

Ephesians 1:13
In Him you also trusted, after you heard the word of truth, the gospel of your salvation; in whom also, having believed, you were sealed with the Holy Spirit of Promise.

Ephesians 2:21-22
In whom the whole building, being fitted together, grows into a holy temple in the Lord, in whom you also are being built together for a dwelling place of God in the Spirit.

Ephesians 3:12
In whom we have boldness and access with confidence through the faith in Him.

Colossians 1:14
In whom we have redemption through His blood, the forgiveness of sins.

Colossians 2:3
In whom are hidden all the treasures of wisdom and knowledge.

Colossians 2:11
In Him you were also circumcised with the circumcision made without hands, by putting off the body of the sins of the flesh, by the circumcision of Christ.

1 Peter 1:8
Whom having not seen you love. Though now you do not see Him, yet believing, you rejoice with joy inexpressible and full of glory.

Romans 3:22
Even the righteousness of God, through faith in Jesus Christ, to all and on all who believe. For there is no difference.

Romans 5:15
But the free gift is not like the offense. For if by the one man's offense many died, much more the grace of God

*and the gift by the grace of one Man, Jesus Christ,
abounded to many.*

Romans 5:17-19
*(For if by the one man's offence death reigned through
one, much more those who receive abundance of grace
and of the gift of righteousness will reign in life through
the One, Jesus Christ.) Therefore, as through one
man's offense judgment came to all men, resulting in
condemnation, even so through one Man's righteous act
the free gift came to all men, resulting in justification of
life. For as by one man's disobedience many were made
sinners, so also by one Man's obedience many will be
made righteous.*

Conclusion

I sincerely hope that we have seen that God's word is equal to and the same as the very presence of Jesus Christ! (John 1) Our Lord is full of lovingkindness and even though we could never deserve the least of His blessings, He has chosen to richly bestow them upon us. Our God is not only ready, but pleading with us as He did with Cain to choose that which is right and pleasing to Him, that we might receive the richness of His blessings in this life and in the one to come. God is far more ready to do good and forgive than man is to receive and accept that which He offers lovingly and freely.

God the Father is working and if we are to be His children, we should be working as well.

John 5:16-19
For this reason the Jews persecuted Jesus, and sought to kill Him, because He had done these things on the Sabbath. But Jesus answered them, "My Father has been working until now, and I have been working." Therefore the Jews sought all the more to kill Him, because He not only broke the Sabbath, but also said that God was His Father, making Himself equal with God. Then Jesus answered and said to them, "Most assuredly, I say to you, the Son can do nothing of Himself, but what He sees the Father do; for whatever He does, the Son also does in like manner."

Shouldn't we follow Jesus' example even as He chose to follow His Father's example? Jesus was at all times entirely submissive to His Father's will. Even in the garden, He knew that suffering, pain and eminent death were upon Him, yet He completely surrendered His will to the Father.

Matthew 26:39&42
He went a little farther, and fell on His face, and prayed, saying, "O my Father, if it be possible, let this cup pass from Me; nevertheless, not as I will, but as You will."

Again, a second time, He went away and prayed, saying, "O my Father, if this cup cannot pass away from Me unless I drink it, Your will be done."

Isn't this the example we were called to follow? Let's always be willing to love, value, and fervently follow all of God's words and commandments.

David's clear and steadfast example of this kind of devotion and Christian living before our God is beautifully displayed in Psalms 119. Please, take a moment to pause right now and read this Psalm. As you do so, notice how many times David says he loves and values God's words and commandments. Soak it up and let it sink into your heart that we may walk even as David did, as men and women after God's own heart.

Psalm 119:128
Therefore all Your precepts concerning all things I consider to be right; I hate every false way.

How easy it is to follow the ways and commandments of men, which can take us far from the truth and wisdom found in God's word alone! Let us daily commit ourselves to be followers of God alone, to daily take up our cross and follow Him and Him only. It is so very easy to fall into the habit of following men and seeking the praise and love of this world, over the praise of God. To let our feelings lead us and not the steadfast truths found in God's Word alone. How good it would be for us as Christians to daily read and meditate on Psalm 119, before we read our Bible for the day.

Here is one of my favorite quotes.

"Man does not search the Scriptures! They do not dig into the wondrous mine of wisdom and knowledge and seek to become acquainted with its contents. Simple, regular reading of our Bibles is the grand secret of establishment in the faith. Ignorance of the Scriptures is the root of all evil!" J.C. Ryle

---

Let's all commit to set aside our feelings and prior ideas and to honor God by honoring His words. By keeping, teaching and living only His words!

Isaiah 66:1-2
Thus says the Lord:
"Heaven is My throne,
And earth is My footstool.
Where is the house that you will build Me?
And where is the place of My rest?
For all those things My hand has made,
And all those things exist,"
Says the Lord.

As we have seen, there is nothing we can give God: it is all His. Only be humble enough to see that all that we do in our Christian walk is our duty before a holy God who deserves our praise and devotion. See Luke 17:7-10; John 14:15; John 15:14.

Remembering that we are to tremble at His Word.

1 Corinthians 6:20
For you were bought at a price; therefore glorify God in you body and in your spirit, which are God's.

Let's choose to glorify God daily in all that we do and speak. Choosing the love and honor of God over the love and honor of men.

Considering all we have learned as we walked through the Word of God, let us spend some time reading and considering John 15. Please, take the time to stop and read this passage in its entirety.

Consider the pictures Jesus Christ creates here for us and how He clearly communicates the importance of our abiding in His Word and commands, and the clear command to work to bear fruit as we do so. Let us daily seek to love our Savior's words and commands, and devote our lives to sharing those precious treasures with the world around us. May the world first see the love, kindness, and graciousness of our Savior living in our lives that it may draw them to our God and His perfect love and goodness!

Does the Spirit of God dwell in you? If not, you are not His. We spent much time in Romans 6 and looked at many other passages that show the significance of entering into Christ's death and coming into contact with His blood. We are taught through these passages that immersion/baptism is the means by which we enter into Christ's death and are clothed in Him. Only after baptism is the Spirit given. Those are not my words; they are a serious and sober warning from our Lord.

Romans 8:9
But you are not in the flesh but in the Spirit, if indeed the Spirit of God dwells in you. Now if anyone does not have the Spirit of Christ, he is not His.

Let's consider and remember when we are promised the gift of the Spirit (Acts 2:38). We are promised the Spirit only after immersion/baptism. Let us with determination and perseverance hold on to the truths found in God's Word, remembering that it alone will be our judge when this life is over. We need not be concerned over the words and judgments of men, because they will not be the standard that we are judged by. This is why it is ever so important that we daily turn our minds to the words of God and fill our minds and hearts with His words and His ways, seeking first Him and His kingdom!

Revelation 20:12

And I saw the dead, small and great, standing before God, and the books were opened. And another book was opened, which is the Book of Life. And the dead were judged according to their works, by the things which were written in the books.

As you fervently seek Jesus and His Kingdom and ways, don't be shocked if you must endure trials and suffering even at the hand of family and friends. Jesus warned us that if we are indeed following Him, we will experience suffering just as He did. But also, we will overcome it just as He did!

John 16:33
These things I have spoken to you, that in Me you may have peace. In the world you will have tribulation; but be of good cheer, I have overcome the world.

It is also comforting to know that there is, as God says, a great cloud of witnesses that go before us and is around us. They have also laid down their thoughts, feelings, and ideas, and have chosen rather to follow hard after God's ways! What a comfort to know that they are cheering us on as we struggle through this life and that we will enjoy the life that is to come with these amazing people.

Hebrews 12:1-3
Therefore we also, since we are surrounded by so great a cloud of witnesses, let us lay aside every weight, and the sin which so easily ensnares us, and let us run with endurance the race that is set before us, looking unto Jesus, the author and finisher of our faith, who for the joy that was set before Him endured the cross, despising the shame, and has sat down at the right hand of the throne of God. For consider Him who endured such hostility from sinners against Himself, lest you become weary and discouraged in your souls.

It is my fervent prayer that you will dig deep into God's word and that you will seek Him with all your might, and that on that *Great Day*, we will all be found **In Him**.

-H. Roye